Did I Give Back Enough?

Arthur Lim
&
Charity Wai

Lions SaveSight Centre (Singapore)

Did I Give Back Enough?

First published in 2009 by World Scientific Publishing Co on behalf of Lions SaveSight Centre (Singapore)

World Scientific Publishing Co
5 Toh Tuck Link
Singapore 596224

ISBN : 978-981-4289-86-3

Design by SinKho Advertising & Design, Singapore

Contents

PREFACE

There are many ways of giving. Apart from donating money, we can contribute our time and skill, or express the spirit of giving through the arts. Even giving our opinions on important issues can help make a difference.

I think Singapore has progressed to a stage where thousands can now, in one way or another, contribute to society. Last year, I was persuaded to produce a book which will encourage all Singaporeans to give. I gathered about 100 individuals for inspiration.

When I was in kindergarten and receiving pocket money of $5.00 a month, 10% would be taken by my mother and given to the Baptist church. By the time I was 12, I disagreed that it should be given to the church. After a year, I was permitted to give in whatever way I felt appropriate. This is interesting as it shows that a child should be encouraged to exercise independence of thought. As life's most important lessons start young, if the government and charitable organisations want Singaporeans to give, they should advocate that a child's spirit of giving be nurtured from an early age.

It is important to recount stories to encourage Singaporeans to put in time and effort, without expecting anything in return. And this is the essence of this publication – that giving should be an act of love, kindness and generosity – we should not expect any returns when we give. We give because we believe it is wonderful to help others.

Let us remember that it is a privilege to be able to give. It is an honour to serve our nation and our university; and what greater value can we have if our money and our professional skills are used to help the less fortunate?

The massive international changes and the global financial crisis remind us that all nations will become poorer and millions in the poor rural areas of developing nations will not have food, shelter or medical care. Those of us who are fortunate to be only slightly affected by the financial crisis are blessed with the wonderful opportunity to do something by giving to the less fortunate.

Arthur Lim

Start Giving When Young

A child should be encouraged to exercise independence of thought and give of his own accord. Life's most important lessons start young.

Professor Tan Chorh Chuan

President, National University of Singapore

Prof Tan, seen here at a lunch held to welcome him, said the university would need boldness, self-belief and conviction to grasp new opportunities. PHOTO: LIANHE ZAOBAO

No.1 authority on Asia: That is NUS' vision

It can be a varsity that influences the future of the region, says new president

By Jane Ng

THE National University of Singapore (NUS) wants to become an international university with a unique Asian flavour.

Laying out his vision for the university for the first time, NUS president Tan Chorh Chuan, 49, said he wants it to use its location and knowledge to stand out internationally and fill the gap left by other established schools.

Already one of the world's best ranked universities, NUS is well positioned to become the No. 1 authority on Asia, he said, and could influence the future of the region.

Prof Tan, who became NUS president last month, was speaking at a lunch to welcome him held at the National University of Singapore Society's (NUSS) Kent Ridge Guild House yesterday.

In attendance were several hundred people, including President S R Nathan, who is also the NUS Chancellor, Dr Ng Eng Hen, Minister for Education, students and alumni.

Kicking off his speech with an anecdote, Prof Tan described how he was too scared to cross a rickety bridge in Pakistan until he saw a local girl run across.

"Crossing the bridge was more a mental challenge than a physical one," he said.

The university was ready to take on the "mental challenges", despite some of them having "daunting bridges".

"We need boldness, self-belief and conviction to overcome obstacles and to grasp the opportunities," he said.

One such opportunity, he said, was capitalising on NUS' expertise in the region.

"As it grows, Asia will also face great challenges," he said. "More research and scholarship is needed to understand critical issues within Asia and to find suitable solutions.

"This will allow us to educate students who not only have an understanding of global issues, but also an Asian perspective and context."

The new NUS Global-Asia Institute, to be established by next year, will focus on broad research issues that affect Asia and will look at how they are interconnected.

Ageing, for example, has implications for health delivery systems and urban planning, as well as financial security issues like pensions, real estate prices and wage gaps, he explained.

Prof Tan also spoke about the need for NUS to prepare its students for "a lifetime of careers".

"It's now not uncommon for people to have 10 to 15 jobs. So we have to change from preparing students for a career for life, to a lifetime of careers," he said.

Training needs to cover not an immediate job but also the ability to pick up new skills and do other jobs, explained Prof Tan.

The new University Town residential college due to open in 2011 is also part of NUS' plans to adapt to the future.

Over 4,000 students will attend small-group seminars and create projects together, while living on campus.

NUS will also look at the engineering and computing undergraduate programme, revamping the engineering course to have a design-focused curriculum and a multi-disciplinary approach.

Earlier yesterday, in introducing Prof Tan, Mr Wong Ngit Liong, the chairman of NUS' board of trustees, described him as a man with a "razor sharp wit, superb memory and a knack for grasping complicated issues and summarising them in a nutshell" who was nevertheless a very modest and humble individual.

Referring to Prof Tan's artistic talents and flair for landscape painting, he said: "As NUS' 'chief artist', today also marks the first of the new strokes you will paint to add new brilliance to NUS."

janeng@sph.com.sg

Giving Back With Passion

Professor Tan Chorh Chuan, NUS President, NUS researcher, clinician and administrator, gives

With leaders and members of the Medical Alumni Association

(Fr Left) Chee Phui Hung, Anne Tan, Health Minister Khaw Boon Wan, Warren Lee, Dominic Leung, Thean Tsin Piao, Moses Lee and Arthur Lim

Addressing members at the Medical Alumni Centre

With leaders of NUS

(Fr Left) Lee Seng Lip, Chew Yong Tian, Tan Chorh Chuan and Qin Shaode

(Fr Left) Tan Chorh Chuan, Wong Ngit Liong, Tony Tan and John Wong

After all these years, I still marvel at the fact that the NUS Faculty of Medicine had been created through a remarkable act of philanthropy. In 1905, the local communities in Singapore led by Mr Tan Jiak Kim, raised the necessary funds to make the medical school a reality. This spirit of giving with passion for the community has endured, even as further development and growth around the medical school has led to the creation of the NUS that we know today.

I experienced this directly as a student. When I was admitted to the NUS medical school in 1979, I was fortunate to have received a government scholarship which allowed me to pursue my studies. In our fourth year, generous financial support from senior doctors allowed a group of us to go on a study visit to Japan, which was truly an eye-opener. Another transformational milestone for me was the two months I spent as an elective student in the Royal Free Hospital in London, made possible by an exchange scholarship.

Over the past 20 years as an NUS faculty member, I have learnt that my experience as a student was by no means unique. On the contrary, I have been touched by the countless examples of people giving with passion to the university as well as to Singapore and beyond.

In NUS, generous benefactors have supported the

(Fr Left) Lee Tzu Yang, Tan Chorh Chuan, Yeo Kong Joon, Johnny Tan, Lim Hong Tan and Wong Ah Long

"When people have a keen sense of belonging to a community, and ownership and pride in its progress and achievements, they would be naturally motivated to step up and to contribute."

Professor Tan Chorh Chuan

studies of numerous financially needy students. Other gifts greatly extended the boundaries of possibilities for talented and adventurous students, by enabling them to pursue their passions and to realise their dreams. Yet others have given their time, energy and talent that have been pivotal in developing a rich tapestry of successful programmes and initiatives throughout the university.

Why do people contribute and give back, to NUS and to society?

I believe the key is a strong sense of community. When people have a keen sense of belonging to a community, and ownership and pride in its progress and achievements, they would be naturally motivated to step up and to contribute.

How can such a sense of community be nurtured?

It must start, in my view, with a collective sense of history and a shared vision for the future that is inclusive, and that resonates with members of the extended NUS community. It is facilitated by good communications and active engagement. Particularly for our alumni and well-wishers, there should be a range of opportunities for those who are interested to partake in and contribute to developments of the university.

With NUS medical graduates

(Fr Left) Arthur Lim, Loh Hong Sai, Teo Choo Soo and Wong Kai Peng

Today, as NUS is making its mark as a global university, the support and help of our extended NUS community becomes even more critical. Generous benefactions have enabled NUS to reach beyond the limits of government funding. Close to $100 million were raised in 2007, reflecting the strong involvement of our community and friends. The physical landscape of NUS has been transformed with many new campus buildings bearing the names of our caring benefactors. Beyond these extrinsic changes, the changing face of NUS also reflects intrinsic changes that are deeper and more enduring such as our intensifying intellectual culture and stronger bonds between our alumni and alma mater.

These are ongoing efforts sustained by the spirit of generosity and giving back. The continued support of our benefactors and friends, and our community will guide NUS to seek and scale new heights as we continue to strive for greatness. I can see that people will never stop thinking that they have given back enough because the more we give, the more it comes back to us. I am including myself as one of those who have not given back enough.

CHAPTER 1

GIVE

Did I Give Back Enough?

"Today more young Singaporeans are undertaking volunteering work, whether in causes they feel passionately about like protecting the environment, or in humanitarian work around the world."

PM Lee Hsien Loong

Prime Minister Lee Hsien Loong

Building a Giving Nation

Excerpt of speech by Mr Lee Hsien Loong, Prime Minister, at the official opening of the National Volunteer and Philanthropy Centre's The Giving Place, 7 July 2008

Every society has to take care of its people, especially the vulnerable groups. Either the state has to do it, or it needs to be done through private initiatives. Market competition and self reliance help drive economic growth, which brings prosperity and progress. But taken to its extreme, the private model means "every man for himself". The poor and needy will then be left to cope through their own efforts. They may be able to get by, but this cannot be the basis for building a nation.

On the other hand, if the government were to take upon itself responsibility for all these social needs, it will have to operate a system of high taxes and transfers, like the European countries. This is an impersonal, bureaucratic model – help for those in need becomes a matter of social administration, not compassion; an entitlement, not something to be grateful for. It would erode the work ethic, leading to slower growth and a loss of economic vitality.

Philanthropy is a better approach. The US has a long history of philanthropic spirit. America's great capitalists of the 19th century, like Andrew Carnegie and John Rockefeller, amassed enormous wealth, but also gave generously. Carnegie had a dictum: "the man who dies rich dies disgraced". Today's billionaires like Bill Gates and Warren Buffett are following in these footsteps, giving away the bulk of their wealth,

"Every society has to take care of its people, especially the vulnerable groups. Either the state has to do it, or it needs to be done through private initiatives." PM Lee Hsien Loong

and in the case of Gates, now overseeing this giving as a full time occupation. As another contemporary billionaire and philanthropist put it, they do not want to deprive their children of the pleasure of making their own money. Younger entrepreneurs are embracing the same ethos. For example when the founders of Google took their company public, they decided that a slice of its equity and profits would go to Google.org, a philanthropic arm. As a result of this spirit of giving, far more hospitals, libraries, universities and welfare services in America are funded by private donations than in other developed countries. Such philanthropic instincts have allowed America's "winner takes all" society to remain a cohesive one.

As a small island-nation with no natural resources, Singapore cannot afford to go the European way. We have to get our people to do their best, do well for themselves, and so help the whole country to progress. So we have gone for low taxes, low welfare, and self-reliance. Our system makes full use of the talent and entrepreneurial drive of our citizens. This has delivered growth and improved the lives of all citizens. But for this to be sustainable, our society has to remain cohesive and stable, and that means that those who have succeeded must feel the impulse to give back to society. The more they have gained from society, the greater their obligation to give back something to their fellow citizens. They must not allow society to be split between the haves and have-nots, and undermine the whole basis for able people to succeed and create wealth in Singapore.

We have not yet built up such a strong philanthropic tradition in Singapore. But many Singaporeans are donating generously to good causes. This started with our forefathers who arrived here in the banks of the Singapore River decades ago, in search of a new world of opportunities. Those who went from rags to riches took it upon themselves to give back to society, and help the immigrants who came after them. They set up charitable foundations like the Lee Foundation and Shaw Foundation. Where there were no temples or mosques, they donated and raised resources to build them. Where schools were needed, they established them to enable the next generation to benefit from the education that they themselves had missed.

The present generation have continued to uphold this tradition of philanthropic giving. We have buildings and school faculties named after major donors or their foundations, like the Lee Kong Chian School of Business in SMU, Yong Loo Lin School of Medicine in NUS, and Khoo Teck Puat Hospital. Singaporeans from all walks of life have also been donating to charities generously, and contributing their time and effort to do good works. Last year, charitable giving to Institutions of a Public Character or IPCs increased by more than 50% to $820 million.

We are gradually becoming a giving nation, but there is potential to do much more. We need more Singaporeans to donate, according to their means and from their heart. This is especially crucial in this era of abundant economic opportunities, yet stagnating wages at the lower end, and widening income gaps. To respond to these trends, the more successful Singaporeans must pitch in to help the weaker ones. Collectively, these individual actions will make our society much more compassionate, and much more cohesive.

Like the American magnates and our own forefathers, we should also encourage successful Singaporeans to deploy

"We are gradually becoming a giving nation, but there is potential to do much more. We need more Singaporeans to donate, according to their means and from their heart. This is especially crucial in this era of abundant economic opportunities, yet stagnating wages at the lower end, and widening income gaps.

To respond to these trends, the more successful Singaporeans must pitch in to help the weaker ones. Collectively, these individual actions will make our society much more compassionate, and much more cohesive."

PM Lee Hsien Loong

a significant portion of their wealth to some larger purpose which they feel committed to, and endow charitable foundations which will continue to do good beyond their lifetimes. But setting up a foundation takes a major effort, so some may prefer to start on a more modest scale, outsourcing the hassle of paperwork and administration. Hence the idea of the Community Foundation of Singapore, whose purpose is to provide just such an option. The Community Foundation will offer personalised advice for high net worth individuals wishing to support worthy causes, and where feasible, pool funds from multiple donors so as to manage them more efficiently. The Government will contribute to the start-up and administrative costs of the Community Foundation during its initial years, with the aim of achieving purposeful and sustained community giving over time.

Besides charitable gifts and foundations, the practice of philanthropy also includes volunteer service. Indeed volunteerism plays an important role in creating a culture conducive to philanthropy. Surveys have shown that positive volunteer experiences in youth tend to lead to generous giving and volunteering later in life. Today more young Singaporeans are undertaking volunteering work, whether in causes they feel passionately about like protecting the environment, or in humanitarian work around the world. The NVPC is looking at ways to further promote volunteerism by creating convenient and flexible options for people to serve in community and non-profit organisations. As more Singaporeans put their resources and skills to use for a larger purpose and to serve a common good, we can build our own tradition of philanthropy and volunteerism, and keep our social fabric strong and vibrant.

"Many Singaporeans are donating generously to good causes. This started with our forefathers who arrived here in the banks of the Singapore River decades ago, in search of a new world of opportunities. Those who went from rags to riches took it upon themselves to give back to society, and help the immigrants who came after them." PM Lee Hsien Loong

Senior Minister Goh Chok Tong

Building a Giving Nation

Excerpt of speech by Mr Goh Chok Tong, Senior Minister, at the official opening of the Cricket Club, 2 February 2007

I hope that one day Singapore would earn the honour of being a "Giving Society". A country known for our philanthropy. Philanthropy means more than just charity. Charity is normally associated with financial help for the needy. But philanthropy encompasses love of mankind and a selfless desire to help others.

To be a "Giving Society", we need philanthropic leaders. These are people who raise funds for worthy causes and encourage others to be philanthropists. They themselves are generous donors. Bill and Melinda Gates are examples of philanthropic leaders. They established a foundation with their funds to sponsor worthy programmes on learning and health. President Bill Clinton is another example. He launched the Clinton Global Initiative to raise funds for HIV patients around the world.

Many wealthy Singaporeans have set up their own foundations to use their wealth to benefit society. I hope that more High Net-worth Individuals (HNI) would put aside at least half percent of their annual income to help others and worthwhile causes.

“I hope that one day Singapore would earn the honour of being a “Giving Society”. A country known for our philanthropy. Philanthropy means more than just charity. Charity is normally associated with financial help for the needy. But philanthropy encompasses love of mankind and a selfless desire to help others.”

SM Goh Chok Tong

“ To be a "Giving Society", we need philanthropic leaders. These are people who raise funds for worthy causes and encourage others to be philanthropists.”

SM Goh Chok Tong

Professor Shih Choon Fong, President of NUS from 2000 – 2008

Give Back? Invest Forward?

Arthur's question, "Have I given back enough?" is provocative, in a way which only Arthur can muster. The honest answer is "No, not enough." And "No, it is not possible to give enough." There is an adage expressing a universally shared value that no one can repay their parents for the gift of life. That being the case, it is not possible to give back enough. For me, having spent a good 30 years away from Singapore, returning home in the mid-1990s to take up an appointment at NUS was an opportunity to contribute to the country of my birth. At the same time, it enabled me to be with my ageing parents in their final years and be by their side when they passed on. I was only doing my duty. I was not giving back.

There are countless benefactors – known, unknown, and unknowable – who help us through life. I recognise that my own professional accomplishments have come about because people I know, and a whole lot of other people whose names I will never learn, made them possible. For instance, my PhD studies were supported by the generosity of many, including philanthropists and devoted alumni of Harvard. I have no idea who those generous individuals who gave so liberally were, and even if I did try to track them down, many of them would likely to be no longer around. Giving back to them is simply not possible. It is as if the person from whom one has received a loan has disappeared or has no interest in being repaid. In my younger days, my mediocre O-level examination results meant I was not eligible for the pre-university track. I went to Singapore Polytechnic instead. While I was there, I had the good fortune to be introduced to a visiting professor from McGill University, Dr Raymond Yong.

He helped me gain admission and take up a research assistantship at McGill. A Lee Foundation travel and winter clothing grant also helped. I owe Dr Yong and the Lee Foundation a debt of gratitude for setting me on my way.

Arthur's question, "Have I given back enough?" is provocative, in a way which only Arthur can muster. The honest answer is "No, not enough." And "No, it is not possible to give back enough."

Professor Shih Choon Fong

The list does not end here. I can also think of a whole host of other people, many of them anonymous, who helped me go to North America – civil servants who processed and approved my visas, university officials who put together my financial aid package – to countless North Americans who helped this Singaporean boy settle in. I have come to understand what the Buddhist tradition means when it describes our lives as being woven in karmic webs, in this case, karmic webs of generosity.

Instead of thinking of it as giving back, I think of it also as investing forward. It is an idea that has been around for a while, the notion that when we give, we invest in the future. When giving to NUS, for example towards scholarships to support students at our Overseas Colleges, I am especially interested in helping those students who might resemble the younger me: someone who does not quite fit the mould, but who has potential and is eager to explore and experiment – intellectually, culturally and experientially. While I have no way to give back to those who gave towards my breakthroughs in life, it gives me great delight to be able to invest forward and help create opportunities for young people to make their own breakthroughs.

Returning to the question of whether I or anyone else has given back enough, the answer must be "No, not enough." We have to recognise that huge needs will always exist somewhere and the poor we will have with us always. It would not make sense to advocate giving until there is equality. Nor should it be giving to address the other person's inadequacy or lack of industry. Rather, we should seek and seize opportunities to invest forward, with a keen eye on creating value, not unlike when making a business investment.

It is my personal belief that in life, one should live passionately, whether that is being passionate about studies, work or relationships. Likewise with giving back as well as investing forward. In giving back and investing forward with passion, I find my fulfilment. I trust too that for the recipient, it goes beyond just money. The true value of any gift may well be in the hope and belief that is invested in the person. In some small way, showing you care and believing in someone and thus encouraging them – I think that is more than enough."

CHAPTER 2

I AM HAPPY

The Story of Lee Foundation

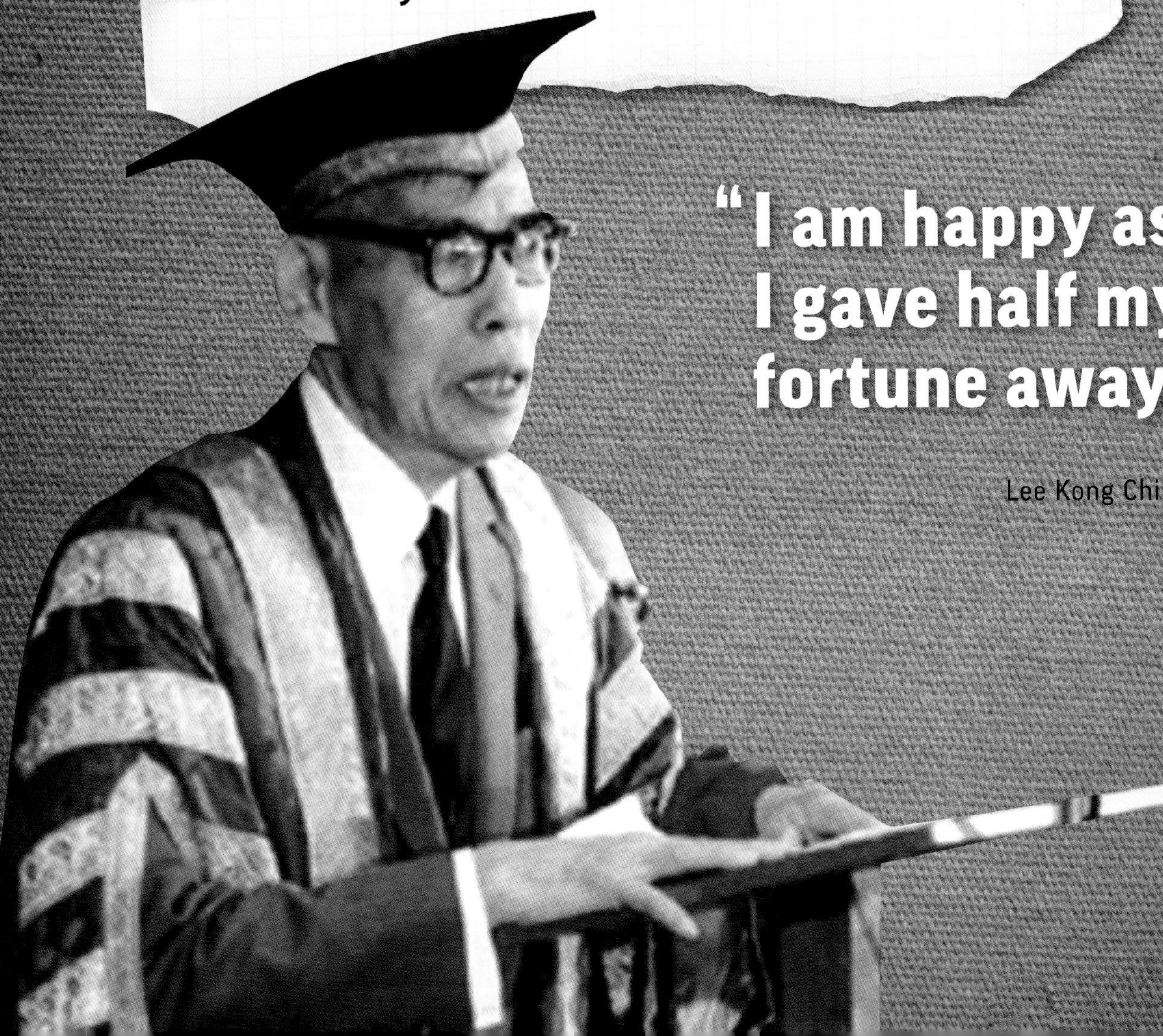

"I am happy as I gave half my fortune away."

Lee Kong Chian

Lee gave money and Marshall gave talent to help

Lee Kong Chian (left) with Malcolm MacDonald (centre) and David Marshall

The Giant Giver

Lee Kong Chian

"Dr Lee Kong Chian did not start his career in business. He worked as a teacher at the Tao Nan School and Chong Cheng School and as a translator for a Chinese newspaper before becoming a land surveyor. He later became Tan Kah Kee's protégé when he joined one of Tan Kah Kee's companies. Not long after, he started his own business and established himself as a rubber tycoon. He became known as Southeast Asia's Rubber and Pineapple King. In 1932, during the Great Depression, which was a time of great hardship in the plantation and tin mining economies of Malaya and Singapore, he played an instrumental role in the merger of three Chinese banks to establish the Oversea-Chinese Banking Corporation (OCBC) that we are familiar with today.

Lee Kong Chian set up the Lee Foundation in 1952 and contributed to various school-building funds and charities – a legacy that the Lee Foundation continues to this day. Many have benefited from the generosity of the Lee Foundation, which has consistently supported cultural, educational and other charitable causes, regardless of race or religion, through good times and bad."

Excerpt of speech by Mr Lee Hsien Loong, Prime Minister, at the official launch of "The Legacy of Tan Kah Kee and Lee Kong Chian" Exhibition, 18 July 2008

Tan Kah Kee

"Tan Kah Kee was fondly referred to as the "Henry Ford of Malaya" – such was the scale of his business achievements. By the mid-1920s when he was in his forties, he had built up a business empire spanning industries such as shipping, agriculture and manufacturing, which had grown to employ over 30,000 people, with 150 offices in five continents.

A strong believer in educational philanthropy, Tan Kah Kee contributed extensively to school-building efforts in both China and Singapore.

Tan Kah Kee was also active in organising the Hokkien Huay Kuan (Clan Association) and made many contributions through the association to provide education for the masses. Today, a part of his legacy continues in the form of scholarships and awards for academic pursuits, such as the Tan Kah Kee Postgraduate Scholarship."

Excerpt of speech by Mr Lee Hsien Loong, Prime Minister, at the official launch of "The Legacy of Tan Kah Kee and Lee Kong Chian" Exhibition, 18 July 2008

Tan Kah Kee's family

Tan Kah Kee (seated) with his family. His granddaughter, Arthur's wife (Poh Geok) stands behind him. This photograph was taken shortly before he left for China.

Tan Kah Kee (left) with Chairman Mao Zedong.

"Singaporeans, especially younger Singaporeans, can learn much from the examples of Tan Kah Kee and Lee Kong Chian – their determination, their commitment to education, and their philanthropic spirit. But the spirit of these pioneers – a willingness to venture into areas that are new and untested, and a desire to contribute to something much larger than oneself – remains relevant to all of us today, and to future generations of Singaporeans."

Excerpt of speech by Mr Lee Hsien Loong, Prime Minister, at the official launch of "The Legacy of Tan Kah Kee and Lee Kong Chian" Exhibition, 18 July 2008

Lee Kong Chian, Founder of Lee Foundation

I Am Happy

There was a man who was always smiling. He dressed very simply, usually in plain trousers and shirt, without any accessories. Sometimes he wore a watch. His overcoat was years old, torn all over, yet he did not see the necessity of getting a new one. His cars were tumbled down ones and he was well-contented with them. Sometimes a stranger in the neighbourhood would ask, "Who is that man in those plain clothes? He is always smiling." The answer would be, "He is Lee Kong Chian, one of the wealthiest men in Asia."

If the stranger pursued the matter further, he or she would find out that Mr Lee became wealthy because he was a good businessman and was one of the top entrepreneurs of his time. Having a great interest in education, he was a generous philanthropist, and so at one point, donated half his wealth to charity. He was one of the first persons in Singapore to donate such a huge sum of money. With that, the Lee Foundation was born.

When people talked to Mr Lee about his wealth and asked why he gave half of it away, he would say, "There are people who are often unhappy because they worry about their money. I am lucky, God has given me a lot of money, so I gave half of it away to help others."

"It is important to know that money is only of value if it is used wisely, especially when it is used to help others. The future of our complicated world belongs to those who believe that helping people in need can move us all forward so that everyone can embrace the joys of life in the coming century. The wise man who is generous will be contented, composed and happy. On the other hand, the foolish man will battle for himself, for power and money, sometimes with intrigue and dishonesty, and will always be full of distress and anxiety."

"I'm very happy... I gave half my money away and I feel very happy. Even if something goes wrong and I lose all my money, it's only half because the other half is in the Lee Foundation."

Mr Lee Kong Chian

Lee Kong Chian's sons run the Lee Foundation

Lee Seng Gee

Lee Seng Tee

Now, Lee Kong Chian had a good friend called Chong Huat. Mr Chong was a rubber merchant and was quite wealthy himself. The two friends often had dinner together. Mr Chong had known Mr Lee for many years, and for as long as he could remember, his friend Lee was always smiling and happy. He often wondered why.

One evening after dinner, Chong Huat said to Mr Lee, "I am a wealthy man, Lee, but I am often unhappy. I worry about my business, my properties and my investments. Tell me, Lee, why is it that you are always smiling and always happy?"

Mr Lee added, "I am happy because I gave half my money away to charity."

Upon this answer, Mr Chong became silent and seemed to be mulling over the statement. Presently, Mr Chong said, "You gave away half of your wealth and you're happy?"

"Yes," said Mr Lee. "I am very happy." Looking at his brooding friend keenly, Mr Lee said, "You worry too much about your money. When you worry too much about money, you become unhappy. Look at me, I gave half my money away and I feel very happy. Even if something goes wrong and I lose all my money, it's only half because the other half is in the Lee Foundation. That cannot go because it's invested outside my own personal interests and it belongs to a Foundation. I'm happy because whatever happens, there is still the other half

"Tan Kah Kee and Lee Kong Chian had much in common. Both came to Singapore in search of a better living, and both started with precious little... Yet through their hard work and perseverance, they overcame many difficulties and became business tycoons. Having prospered, both were moved to give back to society... the infuence and good work of both pioneers persist till this day, through the Lee Foundation and the Tan Kah Kee Foundation."

Excerpt of speech by Mr Lee Hsien Loong, Prime Minister, at the official launch of "The Legacy of Tan Kah Kee and Lee Kong Chian" Exhibition, 18 July 2008

and I'm helping other people. Why don't you do the same as I did, Chong? Give half your money to charity."

Mr Chong's brows furrowed as he contemplated the suggestion. "I'll think about it," he said.

Three weeks later, the friends met again. After their usual dinner, over a cup of hot tea, Mr Lee asked Mr Chong, "Well, have you thought about my suggestion?" Mr Chong said, "Yes, I've thought about it. I did not sleep well for the last three weeks, and there were nights when I stayed awake till morning." Mr Chong looked stressed but he went on. "I have worked hard for 40 years and I was looking into which rubber estates, properties and shares I should give away. I thought of my tin mines and investments in Indonesia and Europe."

"What have you decided?" asked Mr Lee, curious.

"I thought about it and decided," said Mr Chong, leaning back on his chair comfortably, "and I prefer to remain unhappy."

CHAPTER 3

Past NUS President Shih Thanks Four Givers

Of Friends, Critics and Lovers

Outgoing NUS chief says thanks to 4 special men

KNIGHT of the Salmon Order, Dragon Friend, a Man for All Seasons and a Voice of Conscience.

In a touching speech – his last major one as president of the National University of Singapore (NUS) – Professor Shih Choon Fong singled out four individuals by nicknames he had given them and thanked them for making a difference during his 11-year term at the university.

He devoted a large chunk of his Commencement Dinner speech at the University Cultural Centre to the four individuals, beginning with NUS alumni advisory board member Chee Phui Hung, 86 – the Voice of Conscience.

Calling Dr Chee his "harshest critic", the head of NUS spoke glowingly of his courage in speaking his mind.

He said: "It has been said that 'institutions languish when their lovers are uncritical and their critics are unloving'. For me, Phui Hung is both a loving critic and a critical lover."

Moving on to the Man for All Seasons – top eye surgeon Arthur Lim, 74, who is also president of the NUS Medical Alumni Association – Prof Shih cited his work in boosting the university's endowment fund.

He said he was grateful to this "world-renowned eye surgeon who thinks nothing of calling himself a 'professional beggar' for the university",

FAREWELL: Prof Shih will be leaving for Saudi Arabia.

often, he returns home to Singapore, his birthplace...and his coming back to the waterways of his birth invigorates and renews us, just like the Atlantic salmon."

Finally, Prof Shih, who leaves Singapore at the end of the year to be founding president of the King Abdullah University of Science and Technology in Thuwal, Saudi Arabia, thanked his *"da ge"* (elder brother) – Mr Wong Ah Long, member of the NUS Business School advisory board.

He singled out Mr Wong's encouragement, especially during his initial years as NUS president.

"There are moments when one feels paralysed by fear of the unknown...Ah Long reminds me that there's nothing to fear but fear itself," he said. "My Dragon Friend's counsel and encouragement helped me stay the course."

Prof Shih saved his best shot for the 8,733-strong grad-

Commencement Dinner is the finale of our Commencement celebrations. To the members of the Class of 2008, I offer you my congratulations. I am also personally delighted to welcome to our NUS family, our newest honorary graduate, Dr Wee Cho Yaw (below), one of Singapore's foremost bankers and entrepreneurs. Please join me in applauding our newest alumni for their accomplishments and in welcoming them into our fold.

Good Fortune

In his acceptance remarks, Dr Wee spoke of being a lucky man. I too consider myself lucky.

Tonight, I'm especially aware of how lucky I am. Lucky to be sharing my ninth and final Commencement Dinner with you. Lucky to have been able to pursue my curiosity and passion for science. Lucky because of my good fortune of crossing paths with people who saw beyond my unpolished exterior, who accepted me for who I was, and who helped open doors for me. During my Commencement Address last week, I touched on what the Chinese call *yuan fen* – when chance brings people together. They reach out and connect with one another, creating something remarkable. That's good fortune. I shared about the *yuan fen* that brought me – a mediocre student who could not make it into the University of Singapore – to Harvard, where I came into my own and grew intellectually. At Harvard, it was my good fortune to meet smart, enlightened people who saw potential in me, despite my lack of academic credentials and social pedigree. They gave me the space and support I needed to be myself, and thus, to be my best.

Over the years since returning home in the mid-90s, I have had the good fortune to meet many individuals who share a love for our University. I have been privileged that these friends and lovers of NUS have become my friends too. These friendships have not always come easy. Indeed, true friendship often grows out of contention, adversity and heartache.

This evening, I would like to speak of four special individuals, who exemplify for me distinctive dimensions of friendship and embody the best in our alumni family.

Wee Cho Yaw

Shih names four NUS graduates who gave

The four givers who helped him during his tenure as President of NUS. (Fr Left) Arthur Yap, Chee Phui Hung, Prof Shih, Arthur Lim and Wong Ah Long

Voice of Conscience

Etched deep in my mind and heart is my initial encounter with the first individual I shall mention tonight.

He didn't mince words about the University's treatment of its alumni. His words, "You done us wrong" hit me right in the gut. The pain and anger in his voice spoke volumes for how much he loved the University. I had to know: "Why do you feel this way? I want to understand." So began my friendship with Chee Phui Hung, a friendship based on honesty and courage. Friendship, I have found, can grow out of contention. New ideas and fresh insights do not emerge through merely seeking consensus. They spring from contention and vigorous debate. As the Chinese saying goes, – from sparring comes friendship.

When we first met, Phui Hung graded me a "C". Last year, the Medical Alumni made me its third ever honorary member, giving me back door entry to the NUS alumni family and medical fraternity. On this occasion, Phui Hung, my harshest critic, awarded me an "A". This is one "A" I treasure dearly. That's real progress. This progress I attribute in part to Phui Hung's not pulling his punches ever since our first encounter.

It has been said that, "institutions languish when their lovers are uncritical and their critics are unloving". For me, Phui Hung is both a loving critic and a critical lover. I can always count on Phui Hung to speak his mind freely and engage in straight talk, particularly on issues affecting his alma mater and alumni interests. We don't take it to heart. The courage to engage in no-holds-barred, thoughtful discussion is a win for our University. It shows that people are not uncaring, and some, I would say, love our University. I guess you could call Phui Hung a lover and critic, a voice of conscience.

Man for All Seasons

The next individual personifies grace in friendship. Arthur Lim has been most gracious in extending warm hospitality to my wife Lily and me. Charming us with stories of his maverick ways, showing us his art collection and even sharing his vintage wines, Arthur's feisty character and giving nature shine through. I have been told that Arthur plays a mean game of tennis, regularly beating his children at it. I have always felt that his debonair personality and zest for life add colour to our community. Arthur's grace and selflessness have also extended to our alma mater. A world-renowned eye surgeon, Arthur thinks nothing of calling himself a "professional beggar" for the University. When someone as gracious as Arthur knocks on your door, how could anyone say no? Little wonder that the irrepressible Chairman of the Universities Endowment Fund and patron of the Centennial Campaign helped increase our Endowment manifold. Thanks to Arthur, doors to benefactors and potential donors have swung open.

Besides dedicating his life to healing the windows to the soul, Arthur creates food for the soul with paint, photography, and words. Beyond scholarly publications and works of art, his flair for the written word and devil-may-care past inspired the University's Centennial musical, Man of Letters. More than just a man of letters, I think of Arthur as the quintessential "Man for All Seasons".

Knight of the Salmon Order

Let me now speak of a friend who never fails to lift my spirits.

Our first meeting took place in Vancouver, five years ago. At the airport, I was greeted by a huge handmade sign that read: "Prof Shih Choon Fong, President, NUS. Welcome to Vancouver!" Excitedly waving his banner and grinning from ear to ear was Arthur Yap, who leads our British Columbia alumni chapter. Arthur has ventured out into global waters. Ever so often, he returns home to Singapore, his birthplace, and is a regular presence at our alumni programmes. Arthur's coming back to the waterways of his birth invigorates and renews us, just like the Atlantic salmon. You might have guessed I would bring up our iconic fish, especially on this my last Commencement Dinner. I'm also making amends for my omission during the Commencement Address. I didn't want to disappoint our Chancellor, President Nathan, again.

Arthur's love for our alma mater is unflagging. You can always count on him to turn critics around and get people on board. He has shared that: "I am proud to be an alumnus of NUS and to carry the flag of NUS wherever I travel." Arthur upholds the name of our University with pride and honour. Like a true-blue Knight of the Salmon Order.

Dragon Friend

Finally, there is Wong Ah Long my Dragon friend, who is the elder brother I never had. I even call him *Da-ge*, or Big Brother. Ah Long loves our University as few others do. It was his love for NUS, in moments when I found it hard to love, which has made Ah Long such a special friend, both to me and to NUS. Through the ups and downs, my Dragon friend has journeyed with me.

When I took on the job of NUS President, I felt that, as a researcher and professor, I could handle the academic part. However, not being a political creature or one who enjoys administrative routines, my limitations were known to me. Moreover, I knew the job of transforming NUS held both known knowns and known unknowns. What was not apparent at the time was that this job would bring more than its share of unknown unknowns.

And so, as all of you who have handled uncertainties understand, there are moments when one feels paralysed by fear of the unknown. Along comes Ah Long, who freely shared his wisdom and experiences, reminding me that there's nothing to fear but fear itself. My Dragon friend's counsel and encouragement helped me befriend – rather than be intimidated by – the unknowns and stay the course. I hope you will all be lucky enough to have such Dragon friends in your life, who can help you pursue what you love.

Brought Together by *Yuan*, Journeying Together with *Yuan Fen*

Beyond these four, there are countless others, many of whom are here tonight, who have journeyed together with me these past 12 years. It has been an exhilarating journey with a steep learning curve, made all the more meaningful by all the friends I have made. It would take all night to do justice to all who have stood shoulder to shoulder with me over the years and also with NUS. It has been a tremendous privilege, and I'm grateful for the opportunity to serve our University together with you.

Today, NUS is globally respected as a good university. We are now engaged in an endeavour to build NUS as a great university, distinguished by peaks of excellence. Our shared aspiration to grow 10 great programmes in 10 years, or G-10-10, embodies our ambition and commitment to excellence. G-10-10 builds upon the *yuan fen* of friends, critics and lovers drawn together by shared passions.

Passion to unleash the power of imagination, the raw energy for creativity and invention. Passion to push back the frontiers of the unknown. Passion to learn, discover and serve. It is also about a culture of excellence that multiplies the joy of discovery, and celebrates the triumph of the human spirit.

This kind of intellectual and social culture infuses every aspect of the life of great universities. I feel this culture whenever I return to Harvard or Brown, and my heart beats faster. I am inspired by great men and women who make up the soul and spirit of the place. I am warmed anew by the friendships made while pursuing dreams and passions together. Fostering this culture has been my hope for our University.

We, members of the NUS family, have the privilege to build our University as a place of inspiration and hope, offering space and support to pursue aspirations and passions. Journeying together to build NUS as a great university is our *yuan fen*.

Good Wishes for Your Journey

As each of you journeys forth, particularly as you – our newest alumni – venture out, I wish for you the very best of luck.

We are very glad to be sending you, the Class of 2008, off into the working world – so that you can start paying off your loans, and stop spending your parents' money. We also want to remind you that your ties with NUS do not end here; your relationship with the NUS alumni family has just begun.

May you be lucky to find Voices of Conscience to speak critical truths and challenge you to face realities you may be tempted to hide from yourself.

May you have Men and Women for All Seasons lighting up your life with love and grace, showing you what living a full life might be like.

May you also have Knights to lift your spirits, champion your cause, and fight battles alongside you.

And most of all, I wish for you the luck of having Dragon friends, to help you face the unknowns in your life and conquer your fears.

Shaw Foundation Alumni House

Shaw Foundation Alumni House Embraces Givers

The Shaw Foundation Alumni House is located next to the redeveloped Kent Ridge Guild House. Together, they form a huge complex where alumni mingle and network.

Dr Tony Tan, Chairman of the National Research Foundation, was the Guest of Honour at the official groundbreaking ceremony for the facility on 8 May 2006. The Shaw Foundation Alumni House is so named in appreciation of the Shaw Foundation's generous $10-million donation to the building fund. The National University of Singapore Society (NUSS) donated a further $5 million for its construction.

NUS and its various alumni bodies share a collective vision that the facility will be a distinctive landmark providing a focal point for all its alumni to stay connected with their alma mater.

The Shaws – Vee Meng and his daughter, Priscylla, with NUS officials.

Cambridge Scholar gave 18 years of service as NUS President

Lim Pin

Prof Lim Pin became the Vice-Chancellor of NUS in 1981, soon after the university emerged as a new entity following the merger of the University of Singapore and Nanyang University. 19 years later, Sir Alec N. Broers, Vice-Chancellor of Cambridge University, was prompted by the University's expanded horizons to comment, "Prof Lim Pin has ensured the National University of Singapore secured a place among the world's top universities."

In championing the establishment of a strong research culture, Prof Lim was equally cognisant of the practical applications of scientific research. He actively encouraged research and development collaborations with industry. NUS Technology Holdings Pte Ltd was formed in 1995 to commercialise NUS research breakthroughs into spin-offs. As forwardlooking as he was outward-looking, Prof Lim spearheaded the University's global campus initiative that connected the wired community at NUS to the best teaching and research resources in the world.

Prof Lim brought to his office a leadership style described by Dr Tony Tan, Deputy Prime Minister and Minister for Defence, as "fair in his assessment and management of people and thorough in his work". Taking the long and broad view, he cultivated the development of arts and culture as part of the University's pursuit of excellence. The alumni body was reconnected to the alma mater as he welcomed the installation of the National University of Singapore Society's Guild House on campus.

Prof Lim received the University's highest tribute – the Oustanding Service Award – in 2003 for his commitment to service excellence.

With Ivan Polunin

With Harry Elias

With Health Minister Khaw Boon Wan

$100 million to the Yong Loo Lin School of Medicine from the Yong family

Yong Pung How and his wife (Wei Woo) meet Arthur Lim, his wife (Poh Geok) and son (Richard).

Yong Pung How with David Marshall and SM Lee Kuan Yew

It's Never Enough

Lim Soon Hock

Giving And Humility

I still remember the sight that caught my eye and the stench that greeted me... While this happened many years ago, the scene of the *kampong* environment still remains deeply etched in my memory.

That was when I was first inducted into the spirit of volunteerism and the notion of "giving back to the community".

It all happened when I volunteered for a *gotong royong* project in Geylang Serai. I was in my third year of engineering in the then University of Singapore in 1972. There were close to 30 of us from the third and final years, led by a Professor Cheung, on a mission to clean and spruce up the neighbourhood.

I must confess that it took me a while to get used to the filth and stench in the clean-up exercise. But those were little things, in comparision to the overflowing warmth, profound appreciation and immense gratitude of the *kampong* folks, that opened my eyes to the whole new world of giving. I was touched; it was a feeling that money cannot buy.

Simple acts can go a long way to touch the lives of others; as long as it is done from the heart and that you do not expect anything in return.

I realised then that the act of giving starts with kindness and grace, human gifts which are priceless and bring immense joy to others. Ironically, it costs us very little to give, yet many of us are not forthcoming in offering them. Maybe it is because we are moulded by society to keep "chasing the dollar" and that we are shaped into thinking that with money, anything is possible. Or maybe, it is because we just do not have the time, to sit and reflect on the true meaning of giving. Or maybe, we just do not have the time at all.

I have been fortunate and privileged to be presented with a myriad of opportunities to give back to the community through several public and community service appointments, in the fields of education, defence, health, family and lifestyle – all of these on top of my regular work. In all, I have been giving and serving for over 30 years.

I served national service from 1973 to 1995, over a period

of 22 years, having been "recycled" for another tenure. I willingly accepted this as a key appointment holder, and retiring in the rank of Lieutenant Colonel and holding the appointment of Deputy Brigade Commander. I joined the rare few to continue serving national service, when the trend then was for many, who viewed this as an unpleasant obligation, to hang up their boots as soon as the mandatory cycle was completed.

Initially, I too was hesitant as I thought I would not be able to cope with the additional commitments, arising from the multiple appointments, as there was a period of time where my job as the Vice-President and Managing Director of Compaq Computer Asia Pacific, demanded me to travel regularly, but I was pleasantly surprised that I was able to take on these "extras". It was from here that I also learnt that when it was for a good cause, it was always possible to make time and energy, no matter how trying the circumstances were.

As I look back, I know that my time and energy spent were worthwhile, as through these community employments, I was able to not only reach out to and engage a handful of individuals, but the larger Singaporean community. It was and still is a humbling experience for me to be able to give and serve, within my limited capabilities and capacity.

As an example, I was recently reappointed as Chairman of the National Family Council. As a Council, our charter is to build more resilient families and make Singapore a great place for families and children. Other than promoting and celebrating the family through outreach programmes, the Council also gives feedback to the government to shape and refine policies affecting the family, as in the recent exercise to enhance the Marriage and Parenthood package.

With all my community service appointments, I am often teased by many of my close friends and business associates as being a professional beggar; as there is often an element of fund-raising involved. Many of us, who have long been involved in fund-raising in Singapore, be it big or small, will inevitably be given the label. In the last two decades or so, among many of the fund-raising projects that I had been involved in, I counted two as being the most satisfying and fulfilling.

The first was the Universities Endowment Fund (UEF), under the able and inspiring leadership of Professor

Lim Soon Hock, together with his father, helps the elderly

"I realised then that the act of giving starts with kindness and grace, human gifts which are priceless and bring immense joy to others."

Lim Soon Hock

Arthur Lim, and which I served for five years from 1991 to 1996. While the idea was a noble one, for lack of a good and compelling cause, it was a major challenge and awesome task to raise the funds to support the universities and to enable them to scale new heights and break new frontiers. The UEF raked in over one billion dollars over five years, despite the immense challenges and enormous odds.

I remember the Ultra-marathon that was organised that saw many participants in each leg of the round-the-island route, with Dr William Tan leading the way in his wheelchair. It raised a record sum, which I recalled to be around a million dollars. The NUS Engineering Alumni Singapore (EAS), of which I was a former President, was the first to start an endowment fund which raised more than $150,000, all of which was donated to the UEF on a one to three matching grant from the government. I believe the EAS was the first such alumni association to donate to the UEF.

The other fund-raising project which I was involved in was raising $12.5 million to rebuild St Ignatius Church. I was the Co-Chairman of the Fund-raising Committee as well as a member of the Building Redevelopment Committee. I remember the task as daunting and tough, as the campaign was hampered by the SARS outbreak and the economic slowdown that followed. Our deep and strong faith saw us through and we succeeded in raising all the money that was needed, just when the construction was completed, and we were spared the need to seek a bridging loan.

Going beyond the "professional beggar" label, I have learnt that when there is a worthy cause, and we take an inclusive approach to reach out to all, irrespective of income status, in other words, each gives what each can afford, commensurate with each person's means, and the contribution is valued, the goal can always be reached.

We all can give; it is a question of whether each of us has given enough.

I am often asked how I find the time on top of my work, business and corporate engagements. While it is easy to attribute it to efficient time management, which is true to a certain extent, I would stress that when we have the passion, we can always find the time. Work should not be an excuse for not giving.

It is difficult to put a value to the enrichment; it is simply invaluable when we can make a contribution for the benefit of others and we touch the lives of many.

When we are magnanimous with kindness and grace, giving follows naturally, be it in money or in kind or time. It is also important to recognise that one would not be able to accomplish so much without the contribution of others, who believe in the same cause, and are willing to journey alongside one.

One thing is certain, I believe that our world will be a better place when more of us are generous with kindness and grace.

If I could turn back time, I would definitely do it all over again, and more.

Giving and humility – it is never enough.

William Tan leads

Dr William Tan is an NUS graduate, a neuroscientist, medical doctor, Olympic wheelchair athlete and world record holder. In the past 18 years, Dr William Tan has raised $16 million through his 60 ultra marathons, which include pushing himself in his racing wheelchair through gravel and snow from the North to the South Poles. He was the first man to complete 10 marathons in seven continents over 65 days in a wheelchair. On 6 April 2007, he did it again by becoming the first person in the world to accomplish a marathon in the North Pole in a wheelchair over 21 hours and 10 minutes in extreme conditions, including a wind chill temperature of minus 25 degrees Celsius. Only six to 12 feet of ice separated him from the 12,000 feet of Arctic Ocean below.

Dr Tan's life is synonymous with challenges. Polio at the age of two left him paralysed from the waist down. Before the age of 15 when he was introduced to the wheelchair by a paralysed policeman, he had to be carried around, and then learnt to walk on crutches and leg braces. Despite his disability and a humble family background, he went on to become a neuroscientist and a medical doctor, winning scholarships to Harvard and Oxford.

Over the years, amongst the many beneficiaries of his grit and guts have been kidney patients (1987), the Universities Endowment Fund (1993), the Professorship in Geriatrics (2000), the Children's Hospital in Boston (2002), Children with Leukemia, London (2003), the Professorship in Paediatric Oncology at NUS (2005), the "Global Flying Hospital" (2007), Free Wheelchair Mission, California (2007) and Saint George Hospital, Sydney (2007), to name just a few.

William with thousands at NUS Marathon

Leaders of three major foundations – Lien Foundation (Margaret Lien) Lee Foundation (Lee Seng Gee) and Shaw Foundation (Shaw Vee Meng).

Despite winning many awards like the Readers' Digest Inspiring Asians Award, the Commonwealth Youth Award, the Outstanding Young Persons of the World Award and the Distinguished Alumni Award, Dr Tan remains a humble person, always acknowledging the contributions of his parents, teachers and alma mater that had made him who he is today.

Not only does he give back to the community through his fund-raising efforts, he travels all over the world sharing his life story to inspire others to overcome adversity and live life to the fullest. Indeed, as Dr Tan aptly puts it, "There are no dreams that are unattainable for anyone who has the will and determination to redefine what is humanly possible!"

CHAPTER 4

NUSS Johnny Tan Leads 200,000 Graduates in GIVING

Giving Back – Have We Done Our Part?

An Alumni Perspective

Introduction

One of the defining characteristics of a great university is how well its graduates are regarded in the community in which they live and work and how strong a support and sense of attachment its alumni have for their alma mater. And with globalisation today, how well its alumni hold themselves in the global arena is pivotal to the reputation of the university, which is under constant scrutiny.

Alumni from leading universities in the world, especially those in the United States, often have warm affection towards their alma mater. This strong sense of belonging is frequently attributed to the early cultivation of a sense of identity and sustaining it beyond the few years that an undergraduate spends on campus. A common thread is that the alumni's participation and involvement in their alma mater's affairs is broad, and across generations – from the highest level of governance to simple participation in annual collegiate activities. This sense of belonging and inclusiveness makes giving back to the alma mater in whatever form that much easier.

In contrast, the culture of giving in Singapore has yet to take root although there are positive signs in recent years that this attitude of reluctance in giving back is gradually changing for the better. People tend to monetise "giving" as evidenced by alumni responses highlighted in a recent news article "Give to Varsity? No thanks: Few alumni appear to be moved by their alma mater's appeals" published in *The Straits Times* on 16 August 2008.

Reasons frequently cited range from "the sense of

Johnny Tan with Tan Chorh Chuan, President of NUS

Johnny Tan with Shih Choon Fong, former President of NUS

attachment to NUS just isn't there" to "the alma mater does not make them feel like they matter – until it comes time to raise funds". This perception translates into a big turn-off for alumni and the university's appeal materials often end up in the waste bins.

Another article "Just 1% of alumni donate to NUS", published by *The Straits Times* on 30 October 2006 revealed that just 1,452 alumni contributed to the NUS Annual Giving 2005 while claiming that "four in 10 graduates from private universities such as Harvard and Yale open their cheque books".

Yet many Singaporeans who studied in overseas universities such as Harvard and London School of Economics often respond positively and cheerfully to fund solicitations from their alma mater thousands of miles away. Why is this so? Indeed there are lessons to be learnt. Giving is multi-dimensional and need not always be viewed in monetary terms.

Much of what has been covered in the press deals mainly with individual donors and large philanthropic gifts whilst little has been said of giving back from organised alumni groups. So, by and large, have these groups done their part? Like many of the other alumni associations and interest groups that have contributed in different ways, we would like to believe that the National University of Singapore Society (NUSS) has over the years in our own unpretentious way given back in modest measure and meaningfully to our alma mater and the community.

Through this article we would like to share a glimpse of some of these contributions which we hope may be of interest to other alumni groups.

The NUSS Story

Since it opened its doors to the first batch of students more than a century ago, NUS and its predecessor institutions have produced close to 200,000 graduates. This growing alumni community represents the University's largest, and in a sense permanent, stakeholders. Today there are some 60 alumni groups and overseas chapters but only a fraction of this large alumni population takes an active interest in the university's development and progress.

The National University of Singapore Society (NUSS) is the largest organised alumni body of NUS with more than 13,000 members, of which about 75% are NUS alumni while the others are graduates from other local and foreign universities who join as associate members.

Founded in 1954, the early years of NUSS were years of struggles due to the lack of physical and financial resources but thanks to the strong support of then Vice-Chancellor Professor Lim Pin, the turning point for the Society came in 1984 with the completion of a purpose-built Guild House with recreational facilities on the Kent Ridge campus. Membership of the Society grew rapidly thereafter and as our financial position improved, the Society took its first steps in fulfilling its two primary objectives of fostering a lifelong relationship with NUS and the wider graduate community through:

i) promoting the interest of NUS and NUSS members, and
ii) contributing positively to Singapore's political and intellectual developments and helping to cultivate a more gracious cultural and social environment.

Collective Giving To Alma Mater And Community

Since the early 1990s the Society has embarked on a series of initiatives aimed at forging closer ties with the alma mater by way of financial endowments for educational purpose, synergistic partnerships to strengthen bonds between the alumni community and the university including giving faculty members access to its food and beverage facilities.

The first NUSS Professor Artur Ekert of University of Oxford in 2001 with Dr Tony Tan and then NUSS President Mr Lim Soo Hwee

Education

In 1989, NUSS pledged $1.6 million to establish a Student Loan Endowment Fund to help undergraduates in need of financial assistance. When this pledge was fulfilled in 1996, the Society made a fresh commitment of another $1.5 million to endow the NUSS Professorship.

This fund would enable NUS to invite eminent academics from leading universities around the world to share their expertise and knowledge with the university community.

> "Think of giving not as a duty but as a privilege" –
> John D Rockefeller

NUSS Professor for 2004, Emeritus Professor John Habraken of MIT, speaks on "Architecture without Buildings"

The newly completed alumni complex comprises the redeveloped NUSS Kent Ridge Guild House (left) and NUS Shaw Foundation Alumni House (right)

Cultivating The Alumni Spirit

The relationship between NUS and NUSS has deepened considerably in recent years. Graduates' residual feelings of neglect by the University appear to have given way to a greater sense of pragmatism as the University and its alumni community find more common ground to move forward. This is reflected in several very meaningful collaborative projects undertaken by NUSS and NUS. Perhaps more importantly, several of these projects are being or had been driven by volunteer alumni who gave of their time and expertise selflessly in true alumni spirit.

The Alumni Complex

The new $60-million Alumni Complex, a joint partnership between NUS and NUSS, is a shared vision come true. "The Alumni House and NUSS with its Guild House at Kent Ridge can be a winning combination to bring more alumni back to the campus," said NUS President Professor Shih Choon Fong at the Commencement Dinner on 15 September 2002.

The Alumni Complex will create the space and opportunities for the entire university community of alumni, faculty, administrators and friends of NUS to network and participate in events to help build a stronger sense of emotional attachment. Through greater interaction with and involvement of undergraduates in alumni activities, it is hoped that the Complex will help to create one aspect of the unique and memorable experience on campus which recent graduates have found lacking – a common sentiment often expressed by alumni in response to the media.

The Centennial Heritage Run

When the University celebrated its centennial in 2005, a group of NUSS members, with the support and encouragement from the University and its Office of Alumni Relations, and the active participation of students and staff, successfully organised the DBS-NUS Heritage Run.

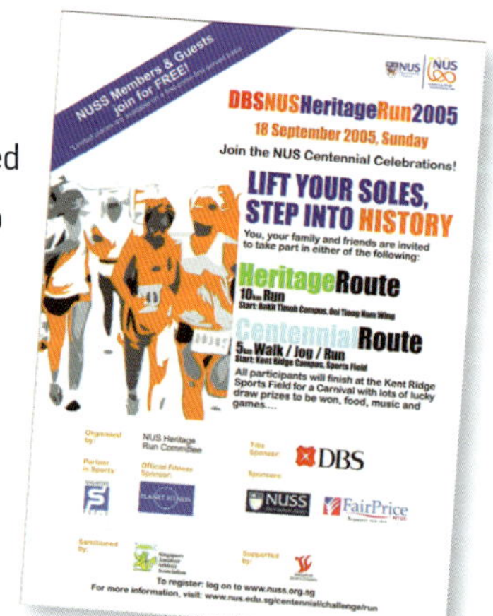

Over 1,000 participants joined in the DBS-NUS Heritage Run on 18 September 2005.

The NUS-NUSS Centennial Golf Challenge on 19 February 2006 involved 1,710 golfers across 13 golf clubs, eventually establishing a Guinness World Record for the most number of simultaneous tee-offs at a one-day event.

Centennial Golf Challenge

The NUS-NUSS Centennial Golf Challenge 2006 was another alumni-driven initiative which successfully established a Guinness World Book of Records for the most number of simultaneous tee-offs at any one-day event. The event received strong support and participation from all the major golf clubs in Singapore.

Supporting Entrepreneurship

In 2003, in support of the University's aspiration of becoming a leading global knowledge enterprise, NUSS readily responded to the University's call to provide seed funding of US$100,000 to help set up the first overseas NUS Enterprise Centre in Silicon Valley, California, USA. This facility has been a speedy and cost-effective vehicle for alumni and student start-ups to gain inroads into the US market.

Welcoming New Alumni

Since the concept of Commencement was introduced in 2000, the Society has been hosting annual dinner parties to welcome each graduating class into the alumni community – an event to mark the start of an alumnus' lifelong relationship with the alma mater.

Since 2000, NUSS has been celebrating the commencement of each NUS graduating class with the NUSS New Alumni Dinner.

NUSS' ongoing social outreach efforts include organising annual Children's Day parties for the underprivileged and celebrating Chinese New Year with the less fortunate.

Community Care

The Society's mission extends beyond giving back to NUS. Over the years it has committed resources not only to helping the underprivileged and less fortunate but also youths and the aged including addressing ageing issues as well as other social concerns that affect the community at large.

The Student Mentorship Programme

Amidst concerns over juvenile delinquency and youth crime statistics, the then Tanjong Pagar Community Development Council (TPCDC) together with Students Care Service (SCS), NUS and NUSS joined hands to establish the Student Mentorship Programme (SMP) in 1998. Through the programme the partners aimed to make a positive difference to secondary school students (or "mentees") who might be at risk by restoring their self-confidence and uncovering their potential.

With funding and Secretariat support from NUSS, a matching grant from TPCDC, NUS undergraduates volunteering as mentors and professional social support from SCS, the programme has been regarded by many volunteer welfare organisations as an exemplary social outreach model to emulate. NUSS' financial commitment to SMP over nine years was approximately $180,000. By its ninth and final cycle, SMP had touched the lives of 647 mentors and 1,175 mentees.

SMP has taught me what is right and what is wrong. [My mentor] brightened my path! And because of his help in my studies, I was named 'Most Improved Student' in my school.

Student Bursary Programme

The Society firmly believes that no able student should be denied a decent basic education because of family or financial circumstances. With the NUSS Student Loan Fund for NUS undergraduates in place, it helped set up a $200,000 Student Bursary Fund in 2004 for NUS High School of Mathematics and Science with a $100,000-contribution and a matching grant from the Ministry of Education.

Creating Greater Social Awareness

Issues connected with Singapore's ageing population did not go unnoticed. In 2007, the Society's Senior Circle partnered University Women's Association Singapore to co-present a Symposium on Positive Ageing: "Golden Years – Glorious Years". The proceedings of the Symposium were later published in a book with the same title.

We have also collaborated with Tsao Foundation to participate in a government-supported community education programme to dispel the myths on ageing issues through the Seniors' Talkshop Programme.

Minister Lim Boon Heng with the organising committee.

Minister Lim graced the Symposium as Guest of Honour.

Then NUSS President Chandra Mohan K Nair and Tsao Foundation President Mary Ann Tsao sign the collaboration agreement on 9 July 2007.

International Outreach Partnerships

Beyond Singapore, our community care group of volunteers launched the first NUSS International Outreach Programme to Cambodia. Under this initiative, NUSS signed an MOU with the Cambodian Ministry of Education, Youth and Sport in December 2005 to provide computers and relevant IT training to teachers and students of selected high schools in Phnom Penh. The programme is a five-year plan and NUSS has successfully concluded Phase 1 of the project in 2007 with the delivery of the final batch of reconditioned computers and peripherals.

This initiative represents a significant step forward for the Society as it seeks to expand its outreach activities through possible collaborations with alumni groups and the university community and perhaps with other regional alumni associations to jointly organise similar projects to benefit the needy in neighbouring countries.

At the signing of an MOU between NUSS and the Cambodian Ministry in December 2005

Intellectual And Current Affairs

Beyond providing the physical backdrop to fulfil the recreational needs of its members, the then leadership of NUSS in the early 1990s felt that a graduate body such as its own has a collective responsibility and role to raise the awareness of its members and the general public of critical issues affecting the nation.

The NUSS Lecture series was conceived as one such avenue to promote wider discussion and debate on topical social, economic and political concerns. At the inaugural NUSS Lecture in 1991, Brigadier General George Yeo, then

PM Lee Hsien Loong in 2005

Acting Minister for Information and the Arts and Senior Minister of State for Foreign Affairs, spoke on "Civic Society". A year later, Indonesian Minister of Foreign Affairs Ali Alatas discussed "The Emerging Security Environment in East Asia and The Pacific – An ASEAN Perspective". 1993 saw Senator Leticia Ramos Shahani, then Deputy Senate President and Chairperson of the Committee of Education, Arts and Culture of the Republic of Philppines examine "Shared Moral Values and National Security". In the 2000 Millennium Lecture, then Prime Minister Goh Chok Tong gave an insightful discourse on "Singapore Beyond 2007". This was followed in 2005 when Prime Minister Lee Hsien Loong shared his thoughts on "The Singapore Elite" – all of which generated considerable interest among NUSS members, the university community and the media.

In between the NUSS Lecture and the NUSS Professorship Lecture series, frequent ministerial dialogue sessions were organised for members to debate on current affairs, ranging from the most recent session on organ trading to regional issues like the political unrest in Myanmar in late 2007.

PM Goh Chok Tong in 2000

BG George Yeo in 1991

Health Minister Khaw Boon Wan discusses organ trading in August 2008.

Minister Tharman Shanmugaratnam considers the globalisation of Singapore in May 2007.

Myanmar's Path to Freedom is analysed in November 2007.

The General Election is discussed in April 2006.

Grace Fu speaks on the Singapore Budget 2008 in March.

NUSS presented The Merry Widow with SLO as part of its 50th anniversary. Patron of NUSS 50th Anniversary Celebrations, His Excellency President S R Nathan, graced the gala premiere.

NUSS productions like Robert Yeo's "Are You There, Singapore?" (1962) and "One Year Back Home" (1980) drew crowds despite modest budgets; NUSS co-presented "All That Jazz" and many other productions with Singapore Lyric Opera.

Promoting The Arts And Culture

The Society's passion and keen interest in promoting the arts dates back to the 1960s. Even with minimum facilities and resources, the early Drama Group managed to put up at least one play a year.

After the completion of Kent Ridge Guild House in 1984, the activity expanded to include production of western operas. Several years later, the Lyric Theatre (Singapore) Limited came into being and this seed that was planted in NUSS has today grown into an independent and flourishing organisation.

Now registered as Singapore Lyric Opera (SLO), it produces top-class operas for the enjoyment of the general public. NUSS is proud to be a catalyst in this successful experiment and continues to gladly render financial support whenever it deems fit.

NUSS presented The Merry Widow with SLO as part of its 50th anniversary. Patron of NUSS 50th Anniversary Celebrations, His Excellency President S R Nathan, graced the gala premiere.

For its support of SLO and its efforts in the promotion of the local arts scene, NUSS was honoured with the Arts Supporter Award by the National Arts Council in 2003, 2004 and 2006.

NUSS Choir celebrates the festivities over Christmas and Mid-Autumn Festival.

NUSS Choir participates in NUSS community events (above) and was invited to entertain an international audience at Singapore Pool's World Lottery Association Congress in 2006.

NUSS Choir's *Malam Singapura* in the Forbidden City Concert Hall.

The NUSS Choir

Started a decade ago by a group of members with a strong passion for singing, the NUSS Choir now performs regularly at community events as part of our social outreach programme. Annual Christmas carolling sessions take the Choir to various homes for the less privileged and oftentimes fellow members are encouraged to join in and help spread the festive cheer.

It has also given performances in the Forbidden City Concert Hall in Beijing, China as well as to audiences in Hong Kong. To promote greater cultural understanding between cultures, the NUSS Choir often opts for songs with a strong Singaporean heritage and identity. Its concert in Beijing, for example, was entitled *Malam Singapura* (or Singapore Night).

Looking Ahead

One could arguably still ask: Have we given back enough? There is always room to do more for the alma mater and the broader society and a lot more can be achieved. NUSS will continue to be guided by its mission and objectives.

Developing A More Systematic And Sustained Giving Culture

From the alumni's perspective there are new possibilities that could be further explored.

As an example of one of these possibilities, there are some interesting avenues such as leveraging on a large membership base to create social enterprises like a co-operative. A percentage of the annual surpluses including attention and sponsorship revenues could be regularly channelled to a Foundation set up to administer annual giving to both our alma mater and other charities and worthy causes.

Promoting Greater Alumni Involvement And Participation

In trying to engender a culture of giving, experience has shown that it is far better to steer clear of hard-sell approaches which invariably put many people off. Investing resources in cultivating a warm spot in the hearts and minds of our undergraduates and alumni will yield better dividends in the longer term. These are challenges which universities and alumni relations professionals will have to grapple with constantly.

How can the alumni community, if called upon, do its part in furthering this cause?

It may be worthwhile for us to take cognisance of some of the best practices of leading universities in the United States with a long history of successful alumni cultivation.

As an example, take Harvard where involvement and participation of its alumni, past and present, seems to underpin the strong affinity which Harvard graduates have for their alma mater. It is common for graduates wherever they might be to receive ballot papers to vote candidates standing for election to the Executive Board or Alumni Association. This instinctively encourages alumni to take an active interest in the university's affairs because their views matter.

Perhaps it might be timely to revisit the concept of the Guild of Graduates where graduates were given the opportunity to elect a certain number of representatives to the then University Council. The University's Guild of Graduates was dissolved in 1980 with the merger of the then University of Singapore and Nanyang University to form NUS.

A revamped scheme could provide for some safeguards to be built in to ensure only those who meet certain criteria would be eligible to stand for election. Any responsible and concerned alumnus would deem it as one of the highest honours to be called upon to serve and give back to the alma mater.

This change, however, would require a fundamental shift in the way the university views its key stakeholders. Not only will it be a watershed in the university's relationship with its key constituents, it will also signal to the alumni community the university's sincere desire to accord the alumni a voice in how the university is run.

Building on the considerable goodwill that has been generated between NUS and the alumni community in recent years, such a historic development would surely usher in a new beginning in fostering a sense of ownership... Perhaps a generation from now, this sentiment would translate into a growing community of alumni, as strong advocates and ambassadors for the alma mater, alumni as education partners, alumni as fund-raisers and alumni as benefactors.

CHAPTER 5
Individual GIVERS

Susie Koh
You Don't Need To Be Wealthy To Give

However, you need to be rich to be able to give – that is, rich in talent, rich in creativity. If you are willing to give your time, your talents and creativity, you can give plenty to society; you can even contribute more money than some of the richest men who are willing to contribute.

As a young woman, I had a calling to help the disadvantaged and to help raise awareness of certain causes that I felt passionate about. I wanted to help the poor and the aged, and also do whatever I could for education and the arts. In a way, I was a failed artist – I wanted to continue painting after my "A" levels, but did not find the opportunity to do so. I also wanted to continue my "ballet", but did not, and I never continued my piano or singing lessons. However, the Arts (be it music, visual or dance) was and still is my passion although I am now working as a Company Secretary and corporate lawyer.

I have decided to use my talents and creativity to help others. I have given my time. I have no money, but I have the ability to raise a lot of money for the poor, for education and the Arts. I can't perform as a world renowned pianist, but I can help raise millions of dollars to fund beautiful music for the masses. I can't dance or paint, but I have the talent to help promote a vibrant arts culture in Singapore.

Susie Koh (left) with Charlene Tan (daughter), Krystal Tan (daughter), Faith Koh (granddaughter), Tiffany Tan (daughter), Eliza Tan, daughter-in-law, wife of James Tan (son).

Susie with Mrs Della Lee and Mr Lee Seng Gee

With some members of the SSO Ladies Committee and SSO Board of Directors (left to right) Susie Koh, Mrs Goh Chok Tong, Mrs Irene Lee, Dr Aline Wong, Mrs Teresa Foo, Mrs Ong Bee Ling, Dr Geh-Min, Mrs Lai-Yong Lawrence, Mr Cham Tao Soon and Ms Eugenia Gajardo

Koh Poh Tiong
Mr Kindness

I would tie a knot on my handkerchief to remind myself to do a good deed each day. You could only untie it after you'd done someone a good turn.

Susie with husband, Koh Poh Tiong

Chief Executive Officer of Asia Pacific Breweries, Koh Poh Tiong, is not just a beer man – he is also a kind man. Recently appointed Chairman of the Singapore Kindness Movement Council, Mr Koh is the quintessential gentleman, and his kindness is reflected in simple acts such as giving his neighbour's son a lift to school to save the boy the walk and bus fare.

Mr Koh's schooling in kindness stems from his childhood days. As a boy scout, he learnt to tie a knot on his handkerchief to remind himself to do a good deed each day. He could only untie the knot after he had done someone a good turn. Today, he makes it a point to "tie a knot" every day. According to Mr Koh, kindness is a multifaceted quality. It could be a reflection of gratitude and bigheartedness, such as being more welcoming and friendly towards foreign talent; it could also be little acts of consideration, such as clearing food trays. As our society progresses rapidly, compassion, courtesy and kindness will help hold together our social fabric.

Known affectionately as the "Tiger Man" in Singapore, Mr Koh leaves APB to helm the F&N Group's Food and Beverage arm on 1 October 2008. Even so, the proverbial "tiger" will continue to be "on the prowl" for acts of kindness further afield, such as Japan, which has the oldest and most influential kindness movement, set up as far back as 1963. Mr Koh's vision is for the Singapore movement to have one million personal membership in time to come. For now, he will strive to encourage Singaporeans to show more kindness without expecting anything in return.

Eunice Olsen

Eunice has always made time for volunteer work such as her piano performance for charities and grooming classes for younger girls. She was also a counsellor with "youth-at-risk" at the Toa Payoh Girls' Home from 2000 to 2004 and the Andrew and Grace Home for troubled teens since 2002.

She also volunteered at the Eurasian Association from 2001 to 2003 and currently serves as a committee member on the Kebun Baru Youth Executive Committee, which is part of the People's Association Youth Movement (PAYM). She is actively involved in PAYM's sister organisation – T-Net Club – that helps teenagers between 11 and 16 develop their creativity.

In 2005, Eunice spoke and participated at many events such as the National Volunteer & Philanthropy Centre Conference, and the Singapore Volunteer Corps Camp. She also became ambassador for the Red Cross National Blood Programme, National Library and Beyond Social Services.

In the same year, she started "Water for Living, Books for Learning" – a humanitarian project to build libraries and provide orphanages and schools in Cambodia, Laos and Kalimantan with water-filtration systems. This has now become the flagship project of "Knowledge in Developing Societies (KIDS)", an organisation she co-founded. Ms Olsen also serves as a member on various committees such as the Citibank–YMCA Youth-For-Causes Committee and the Council for Formation of Alumni for Girls' and Boys' Home.

In 2005, as a Nominated MP, Ms Olsen had a national platform to serve the community and reach out to the youth of Singapore. On top of that, as a young alumnus, she also returns to serve on the NUS Alumni Advisory Board.

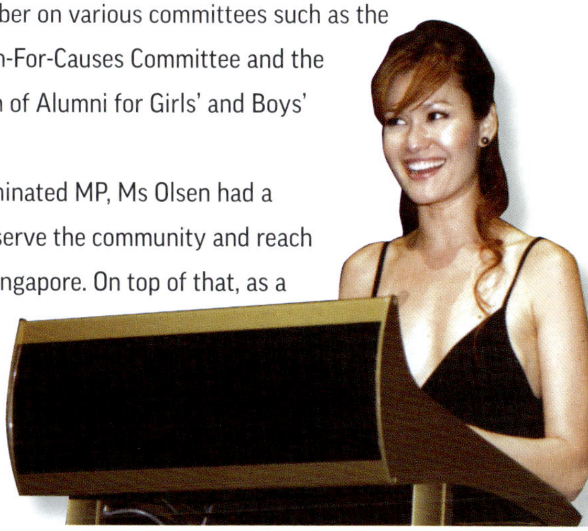

Woffles Wu

Think of plastic surgery in Asia and one name immediately springs to mind – Dr Woffles Wu. This innovative and exciting plastic surgeon from Singapore has for years been the name on the lips of men and women seeking aesthetic perfection. Armed with an impeccable eye for beauty, balance and harmony, Dr Wu has reinvented and promoted the concept of Non Surgical Facial Rejuvenation (NSFR). He is today one of the most sought after speakers around the world on this topic and his invention, the WOFFLES LIFT, which helps women achieve facial rejuvenation.

Despite his hectic schedule, one thing this fascinating Renaissance surgeon has not given up is painting and sculpting. A hobby he started in his teens, Dr Wu has gone on to exhibit his unique style of Psychoerotic paintings in Taiwan and Singapore and continues to use his art to raise money for charity.

James Wong

Rev Canon Dr Wong has been in active Christian service for 50 years. He has served on many Christian organisations which include the Scripture Union, Graduates Christian Fellowship, the National Council of Churches, the Evangelical Fellowship of Singapore and the Lausanne Committee on World Evangelisation.

Since 1986, he has been the Founder-President of the annual Festival of Praise. He has planted several churches both in Singapore and Indonesia.

Currently he serves as the Honorary National Director for Crown Financial Ministries and the Crusade for World Revival which was founded by the late Selwyn Hughes.

Alan Coleman

Alan Coleman is currently a Principal Investigator in the A*STAR Institute of Medical Biology and also Executive Director of the Singapore Stem Cell Consortium. His research will involve the differentiation of human and mouse embryonic or embryonic-like (induced pluripotentia) stem cells that harbour deleterious mutations known in humans to cause distinctive pathological conditions. Neurodegenerative disease will comprise a major focus.

Tan Chin Tiong

Tan Chin Tiong was Provost at the Singapore Management University. He is a co-author of *Marketing Management: An Asian Perspective, Asia's Tao of Business* and *New Asian Emperors*. He has published in *Journal of Consumer Research, Journal of International Business Studies, International Marketing Review* and other international journals and conference proceedings. He sits on the boards of several companies and committees of government agencies. He is academic advisor to the Singapore Airlines' Management Centre, and has consulted for companies like Acer Computer, Altron Group, Inchcape and Singapore Telecom.

Arthur greeting Chin Tiong and his wife, Josephine.

Seet Keng Yew (2nd from left) with Tony Chew, Arthur and Joy Balakrishnan

Seet Keng Yew

Seet Keng Yew is the grandson of the late banker and philanthropist Khoo Teck Puat whose foundation donated S$125 million towards building and funding the hospital in Yishun named after Mr Khoo.

Richard Eu

Richard Eu is Group CEO of the Eu Yan Sang Group. Prior to this, he worked in merchant banking, investment management, stock broking, computer distribution and venture capital before becoming the Group General Manager of Eu Yan Sang Holdings Ltd (EYSH) in 1989. EYSH was the owner of the Eu Yan Sang business in Singapore and Malaysia at that time. In 1993, Richard organised a management buyout of the business and in 1996 it was merged with the Eu Yan Sang business in Hong Kong, forming the Eu Yan Sang International Group, as it is today. Richard is an Independent Director of Broadway Industrial Group Limited, Chairman of the Governing Council of Singapore Institute of Management and Chairman of Harry's Holdings Limited. Richard graduated with a Bachelor's degree in Law from London University, UK. Apart from his business interests, he is also involved in community projects and non-profit organisations. He served as Chairman of the Community Chest from 1992 to 2000.

Dick Lee

The Dick Lee phenomenon started in 1971 when, at the age of 15, Dick participated in various talent contests with the groups, Harmony and Dick and the Gang (teaming with his siblings). His first album, LIFE STORY, featuring his own compositions, was released in 1974.

Dick celebrated the 30th anniversary of his career in 2004 with the release of a five-CD compilation as well as his autobiography THE ADVENTURES OF THE MAD CHINAMAN. He also created DICK LEE'S SUNSHINE PROJECT, a charity for handicapped children and youth counselling centres, in conjunction with the Community Chest of Singapore.

More recently, Dick was one of the judges for the Singaporean incarnation of the popular IDOL platform, and was the host for the first ever High Definition Television programme FINER SIDE (2006).

Dick received the Singapore Cultural Medallion in 2005.

Jennie Chua

Jennie Chua is President and Chief Executive Officer of The Ascott Group. She was the President and Chief Executive Officer of Raffles Holdings Limited from April 2003 to January 2007. Currently, she sits on the Board of several companies, and serves on various local and international government and community service boards and committees.

Ms Chua chairs the Singapore Film Commission, Tourism Industry Skills and Training Council, Community Chest of Singapore and Sentosa Cove. She has been honoured with other accolades and awards, including two Singapore National Day awards, 25 Stars of Asia 2003, Person of the Year – Asia Pacific (Hotel) 2002, National Productivity 2002, Pacific Area Travel Writers Association Hall of Fame 2000, Hotelier of the Year 1999, Woman of the Year 1999, Champion of the Arts 1999 and Independent Hotelier of the World 1997.

Wu Guanzhong

In September 2008, Wu Guanzhong donated 113 artworks worth an estimated value of SGD 66 million to the Singapore Art Museum. This gift is the highest donation value that has been made to any museum in Singapore to date.

Born on 29 August 1919 in Yixing, Jiangsu Province, Wu Guanzhong is a leading Chinese painter, art educator and essayist of the 20th century. He completed his studies in Chinese and Western painting in the National Arts Academy of Hangzhou under such teachers as Pan Tianshou and Lin Fengmian. In 1947, he travelled to Paris on a government scholarship to study at the Ecole Nationale Superieure des Beaux Arts, where he primarily studied modern western art. Upon his return to China in 1950, he taught at the Central Academy of Art in Beijing, encouraging students to assimilate and fuse traditional Chinese art with western forms in order to discover their own style. The pro-form theory he espoused was vital in the development of China's art away from subject-centricism in social realism.

By the early 1980s, his own artistic style had reached the acme of perfection, establishing a painterly language that is unique and truly his own. Mr Wu's artistic principles are balanced between the individual and society, as well as between formal beauty and the awareness of mass receptivity.

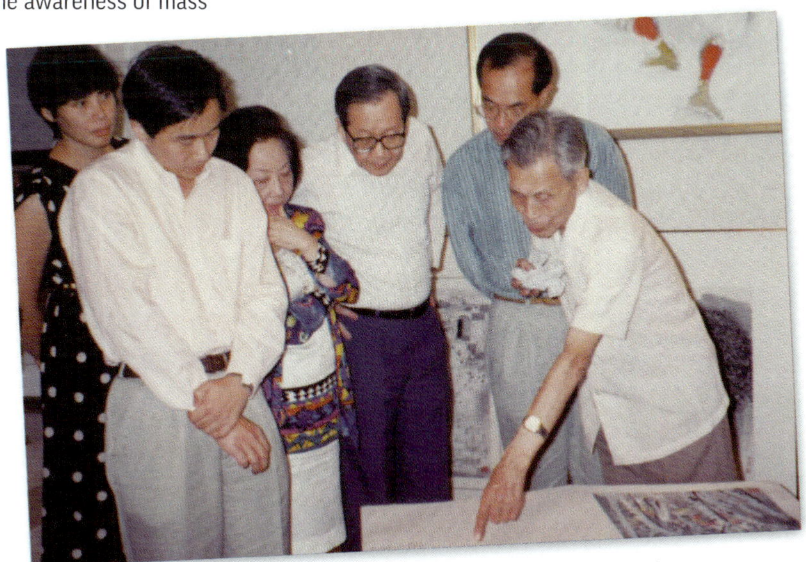

With Minister George Yeo (then Minister for Information and Arts), Lim Pin (former Vice-Chancellor, NUS), Betty Lee (Lee Foundation) and others.

Wang Gang Wu

Professor Wang is the Director of The East Asian Institute in the National University of Singapore and the Deputy Chairman of the Chinese Heritage Centre from 2001. His previous appointments include Vice-Chancellor, University of Hong Kong from 1986 to 1995 and Chairman, Institute of East Asian Political Economy from 1996 to 1997.

He is also an active participant of numerous boards both international and local. His publications include *A Short History of the Nanyang Chinese*, *The Cultural Background of the Peoples of Malaysia: Chinese Culture, China* and *the Chinese Overseas* and *The Chinese Way: China's Position in International Relations*. He has also received various awards and honours recognising his contributions.

GK Goh

Goh Geok Khim is Chairman and Non-Executive Director of Boardroom Limited, and Executive Chairman of G.K. Goh Holdings Ltd. Mr Goh is also Chairman of the Boards of Temasek Foundation (CLG) Limited, The National Museum of Singapore, and Federal Iron Works Sdn Bhd. In addition to these appointments, he is also a member of the National Heritage Board, and a Non-Executive Director of Lam Soon (M) Bhd.

In 1996, he donated The William Farquhar Collection of Natural History Drawings to the National Museum. Mr Goh had purchased the drawings, bequeathed to the Royal Asiatic Society by Farquhar, at a Sotheby's auction in 1993. Mr Goh holds a Bachelor of Science degree in Civil Engineering from the University of Colorado.

Han Thien Fong

Han Thien Fong has made many indelible Lionistic contributions in the Singapore Host Lions Club, District 308-A1, MD308 and Lions Clubs International. His best contribution is in training, developing and mentoring the many Lion leaders and members in Singapore and in MD308. Over the years, Lion Han has continued to serve the community tirelessly and with a high level of commitment. His first project was the Children's Day Party for underprivileged children in 1983. His latest project is the Lion SaveSight Centre (Singapore).

Kwek Hong Png

The late Kwek Hong Png was a classic overseas Chinese success story. He left Fujian province as a penniless teenager with his three brothers, arriving in Singapore in 1928 and later founding the Hong Leong group here. A noted philanthropist, his family donated $2.8 million to the Asian Civilisations Museum (ACM). The Kwek Hong Png China Gallery at the ACM is named after him.

Koh Boon Hwee

Koh Boon Hwee is the Executive Chairman and CEO of Sunningdale Tech Ltd.

He is currently the Executive Director of MediaRing Ltd, and Chairman of DBS Group Holdings Ltd and DBS Bank Ltd. Mr Koh is also the Chairman of the Nanyang Technological University's Board of Trustees, and serves as a Director of Agilent Technologies, Inc in the United States.

Mr Koh holds a degree in Mechanical Engineering (First Class Honours) from the Imperial College of Science and Technology, University of London, and an MBA (Distinction) from the Harvard Business School.

Ng Teng Fong

Ng Teng Fong is a Singapore real estate billionaire. His family owns the development corporation Sino Group. Mr Ng made his fortune with the help of one of Singapore's early billionaires, Eliya Thamby. Despite his fortune, he has a reputation for leading a frugal and unostentatious lifestyle. Today, he is one of Hong Kong's largest real estate developers and he is one of the largest landholders of Far East Organisation in Singapore. In 2008, Far East Organisation generously contributed the space to set up NVPC's The Giving Place.

Oei Hong Leong and his beautiful wife, Angela, donate millions

Oei Hong Leong donates $2 million to support Goh Chok Tong's proposal for the NextGen Leadership Foundation.

Besides Tan Kah Kee Foundation and Lee Kong Chian Foundation, the Shaw Foundation, Ng Teng Fong and other established givers, a new generation has emerged. Of the many foundations, Oei Hong Leong Foundation has a strong potential to lead private philanthropy in Singapore.

Oei Hong Leong bets on AIG for LKY School

WHO dares wins, works as a motto for Britain's elite SAS forces and it is likely to work wonders for the Lee Kuan Yew School of Public Policy, thanks to a bold share market gamble by tycoon Oei Hong Leong.

Mr Oei bought one million American International Group (AIG) shares on Tuesday when the stock was in freefall and many investors were bailing out of the giant insurer.

He told The Straits Times that he will donate the shares, which have already shot up in value, to the school to mark Minister Mentor Lee Kuan Yew's 85th birthday, which fell on Tuesday.

Mr Oei's gambit on Tuesday was about as daring as you can get given the onslaught of bad news swirling around AIG.

"I had a gut feeling," he said.

But it was still a nerve-wracking day. AIG shares lost as much as 70 per cent on the opening bell on Wall Street to plunge to US$1.25 before swiftly ratcheting upwards.

Mr Oei bought in on the upswing and landed his parcel for US$1.80. By the close of trading they were more than double that – US$3.75.

Yesterday, the shares opened at US$3.10, though they weakened later to US$2.

Mr Oei's gamble was not based only on a gut feeling. He looked hard at the unfolding AIG crisis and calculated that the firm was just too big and important to be allowed to fail.

AIG insures a wide range of products with many different counterparties, which likely promoted the US government to step in yesterday with a US$85 billion bailout.

Mr Oei was also confident of AIG's financials. "Unlike an investment bank, which does not have many assets and acts like traders, insurance companies have more assets and have quite a conservative policy towards accounting for them," he reasoned.

But while the AIG deal paid off, Mr Oei believes the financial turmoil represents "only the end of the beginning".

It is not just the sub-prime mortgage market which is at risk but all mortgages as property prices are falling while US unemployment is rising, he said.

"The game is over. Banks don't trust each other and won't even lend to each other. They find it difficult to raise capital because the big investors are not willing to fund them anymore. Soon they will have to cut their asset portfolios and sell their assets to raise funds, so it will be a bloodbath."

Last week, Mr Oei donated $2 million to the NextGen Leadership Foundation. The scheme, which encourages young people to lead grassroots or welfare organisations, was unveiled last month by Senior Minister Goh Chok Tong.

LEE SU SHYAN

Stefen Chow

I profess that I have never given back enough. When I was first asked by Prof Arthur Lim to contribute to this book, I was initially puzzled as to why I was chosen. In my undergraduate years, I was part of the Eusoff Voluntary Corps that brought food and laughter to a group of old folks in a quiet part of Chinatown every Saturday morning. I was also a counsellor at a Boys' Home. Since becoming a professional photographer about three years ago, I have been involved in a few community projects. One of these was the "Water for living, books for learning" project in Cambodia and Laos. Part of this project was to collect children's books from Singaporeans and contribute them as learning resources to schools and communities in the two countries. It was a simple and relatively straightforward plan that could potentially bring benefits to many people. Over the years, I have learnt that giving should not be about awards or recognition, but something that comes from the heart and the genuine desire to make positive changes.

Kua Harn Wei

Kua Harn Wei belongs to a rare breed of sportsmen who excel equally in the sports and in their academic pursuits. Since his participation in his first Ironman World Championship held in Hawaii in 1997, Dr Kua has moved on to become the first Singaporean to complete a Double Ironman World Championship (twice the Ironman distance) in 2003. In 2005, he set a new Asian record in the Quintuple Ironman World Championship held in Mexico. After five gruelling months racing around the world between July to November 2008, Dr Kua established himself as the second top ultratriathlete in the world and also raised more than $600,000 for the Shaw Foundation Alumni House's student and alumni programmes.

Peter Lee and wife, Janice, and daughters: Clarissa, Sandra, Patricia and Sherly

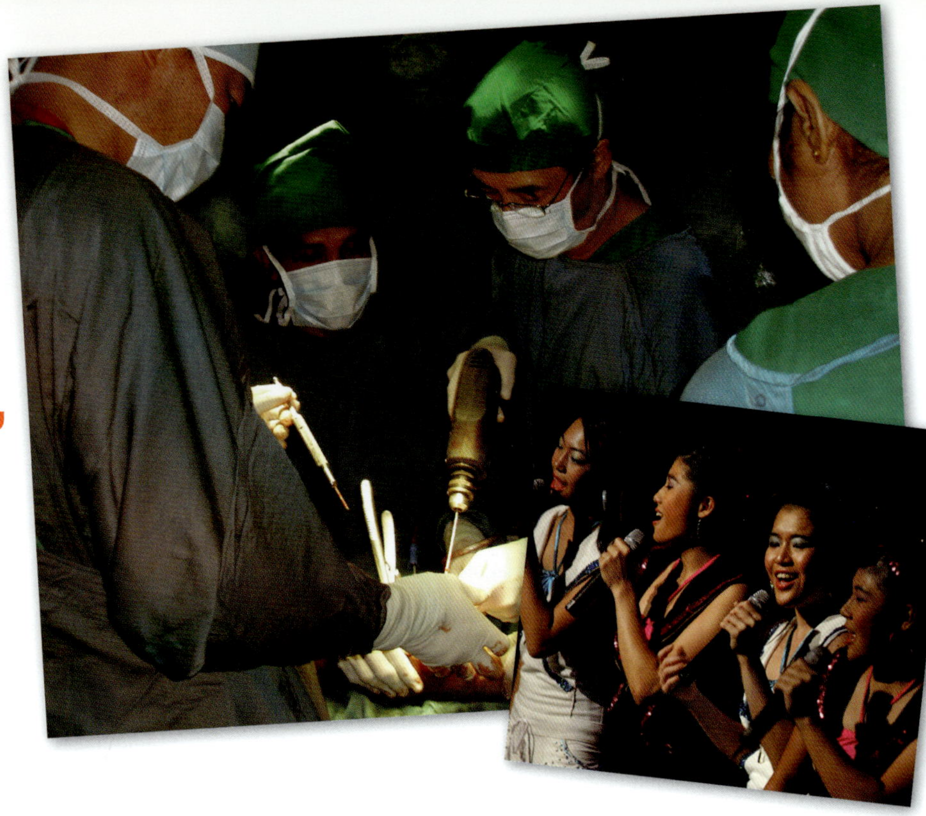

THE STRAITS TIMES FRIDAY DECEMBER

Family give up ski trip to help orphans in Medar

Medical doctors and their four daughters to be part of Mercy Relief project

BY JEREMY AU YONG

THIS holiday season, rather than zip down the ski slopes of Whistler in Canada, the Lee family will work at orphanages in Indonesia.

Orthopaedic surgeon Peter Lee, his wife and three of their daughters will head to Medan, Indonesia as part of a Mercy Relief entourage to help orphans in the area.

Said Dr Lee: "There's a lot of satisfaction in helping the needy. It's something we've wanted to do for a long time.

"I also wanted the girls to see the other side of life. I want them to realise other people are suffering. They are very used to the comfort here."

His three older daughters — Patricia, 18, Sheryl, 16, and Sandra, 14 — left Singapore two days ago with about 50 other volunteers from the welfare organisation on a two-week expedition to refurbish four orphanages.

Dr Lee and his wife, general practitioner Janice Khoo will join the contingent next week to offer free medical screening at the orphanages. Their youngest daughter Clarissa, aged nine, is too young to volunteer but will tag along with her parents.

The visit to the impoverished villages of Medan will be a change for the family.

The girls will be put up in spartan wooden guest houses with no TV or air-conditioning. They will also have to roll up their sleeves to repair roofs, paint walls and lay bricks.

The Lees live in a luxurious home, made up of two adjoining condominium units in Bayshore Park. The family have also been known to take up to four holidays a year, living it up in five-star resorts equipped with private jacuzzis.

"We normally take multiple trips during the holiday season," admitted Dr Khoo.

"We go skiing in Whistler, visit relatives in Australia and then we may go on golfing holidays around the region."

This year, however, the trip to Medan will be the only one. The family will even miss their customary Christmas Day bash as they arrive back in Singapore only on the night of Dec

Despite the sacrifice girls said they are th about the trip.

Said Sandra, who is in ria Junior College's integ programme: "I'm quite ex about it. I've always want do charity, not just donate

In fact, the four sisters a enthusiastic about the pro they organised a fund-rai concert to raise money. two weeks, they practised with a professional voice co and dance choreographer.

The concert, held last Fri and attended by about friends and family membe raised over $8,000 for Me Relief's humanitarian projec

For more information Mercy Relief and its projec visit www.mercyrelief.org call 6332-6320.

Would you give a Mercedes away?

I won this Mercedes but I gave it away to charity.

Janice Lee

Donald Tan

He pushed eye research in Singapore from almost nothing to the world stage.

Donald Tan exhibits the rare combination of a talented, dedicated and caring clinician; a surgeon of the highest calibre; and an active researcher interested and skilled in clinical and basic research. His particular interests have been in ocular surface disorders, especially the aetiology of pterygium at the cell and molecular level; and in corneal transplantation, particularly the problems associated with corneal graft rejection. He spearheaded the development of corneal services at the SNEC, reorganising the corneal transplantation service and establishing the Singapore Eye Bank. Currently, he is actively involved in national initiatives in tissue banking.

In 2006, Professor Tan was awarded the first Minister for Health Award For Outstanding Performance In Public Health in Singapore for leading the Singapore team which first identified the cause of the global outbreak of Fusarium keratitis.

Putting Words into Action – Prof Donald Tan seen here running in a marathon to raise funds for the Singapore Eye Bank.

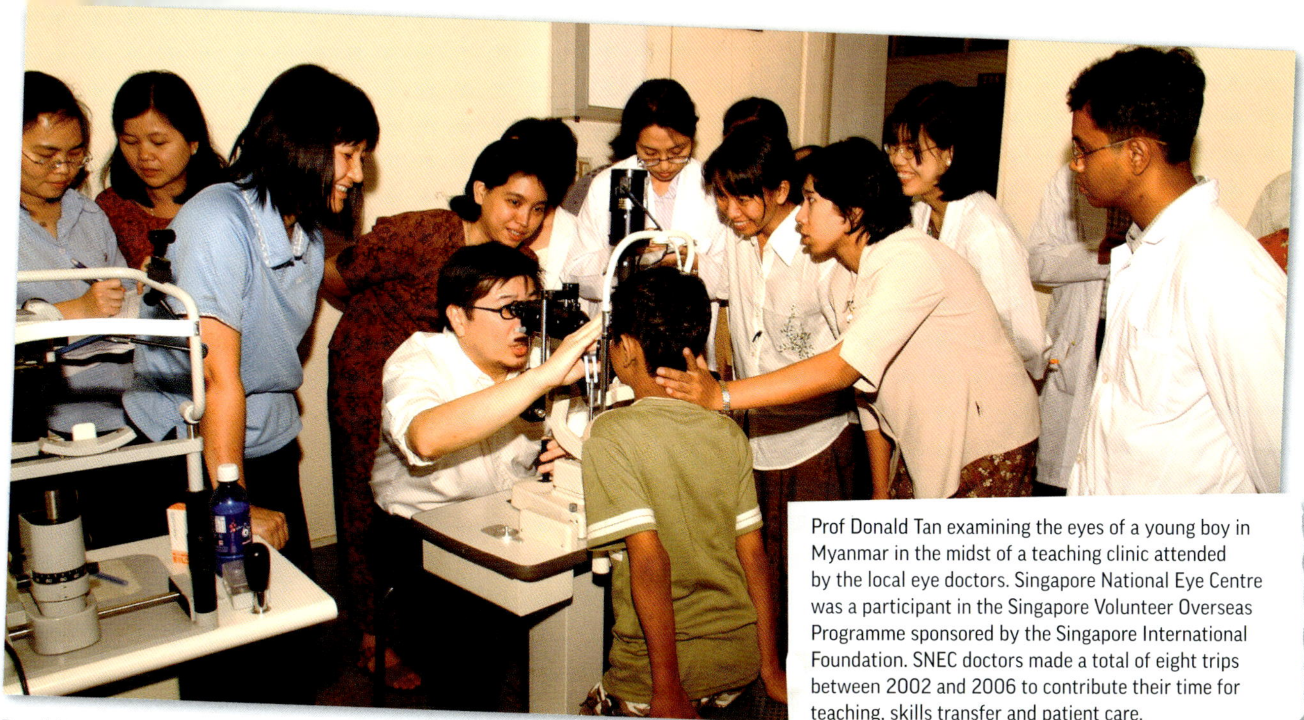

Prof Donald Tan examining the eyes of a young boy in Myanmar in the midst of a teaching clinic attended by the local eye doctors. Singapore National Eye Centre was a participant in the Singapore Volunteer Overseas Programme sponsored by the Singapore International Foundation. SNEC doctors made a total of eight trips between 2002 and 2006 to contribute their time for teaching, skills transfer and patient care.

Donald in Myanmar

Wallace Foulds

His advice has been invaluable. His leadership in ocular research will always be remembered.

Wallace Foulds is well known to ophthalmologists in the Asia-Pacific. He is internationally regarded as a world-famous ophthalmic researcher. He came to answer Professor Arthur Lim's call to help spearhead clinical and basic ophthalmic research in Singapore.

Prof Foulds has been professionally active in the Asia-Pacific area for many years, having been a frequent guest lecturer in Asia, including India, Pakistan, Malaysia, Japan, Hong Kong, and Singapore. He has been involved in the reorganisation of eye services in Hong Kong and the Prevention of Blindness Programme in India.

He is Research Adviser to the Singapore National Eye Centre (SNEC) and sits on the Advisory Board of Singapore Eye Research Institute. He is

also Visiting Professor of the Department of Ophthalmology, National University of Singapore.

Chew Sek Jin

"There are a lot of capable people, but few are both capable and respectable. Sek Jin was extremely capable and well respected by his patients and those who had the chance of working with him. He was a visionary, selfless and both a good team leader as well as a team player," said Professor Dennis Lam, colleague and long time friend of the late Prof Chew Sek Jin.

The late Prof Chew Sek Jin was the first of us to acquire MS and PhD degrees. In 1993, he left Singapore to pursue a PhD in the USA in the midst of a promising clinical career. As the first full-time medical staff of the Department of Ophthalmology in the National University Hospital (NUH), he had blazed the trail by devoting his career to full-time research, leading by example in showing how research should and must be integral to the future of ophthalmology in Singapore.

Professor Chew died of a brain tumour when he was 39.

In those early days, he worked day and night writing grant proposals to the National Medical Research Council (NMRC), recruiting scientists locally and overseas, and cajoling medical students to participate in projects. At the same time, he was networking with industry and overseas research collaborators to build a name for Singapore as the potential hub for eye research in Asia.

It was at one of those overseas meetings that Sek Jin fell ill, collapsed, and was found to have an inoperable brain tumour. Most people would have resigned themselves to fate and would have given up, but not Sek Jin. He worked even harder and faster, knowing that he was living on borrowed time.

Elizabeth Choy

Better known in Singapore as a war heroine, Elizabeth Choy, and her husband were jailed and tortured by the Japanese Military Administration Department for helping to pass food, medicine and messages to British prisoners of war during the Japanese Occupation. Her psychological resilience helped her to endure the interrogations by her Japanese captors. After the war, Mrs Choy was awarded the Order of the British Empire (OBE) in recognition of her valour during the Japanese Occupation of Singapore.

In her reflection on the lessons learnt from the war, she said, "My values are quite changed. I am no more materialistic, even to this day. Never mind if I have no mansion, no diamonds... still I'm happy."

Foremost, Mrs Choy was a natural and dedicated educator for 40 years. She started teaching first at St. Margaret's School and later St. Andrew's School; and was the first principal of the Singapore School for the Blind in 1956. For her years of service in education, she was awarded the Long Service Award by the Singapore Government in 1973. She retired from St. Andrew's in 1974.

Koh Choon Joo

"Money is not everything to me, enough is enough."

He was a successful lawyer who preferred to live a reclusive life. But he came foward to donate $2 million to the Universities Endowment Fund when he was approached. CJ Koh, as he was better known, was also a self-taught artist and poet. "Money was not everything to him, enough was enough," said Susie Koh, who was instrumental in bringing together CJ Koh and the university fund.

The reclusive Mr Koh, a retired lawyer and former Honorary Magistrate, in a photograph taken in 1979.

By Tan Hsueh Yun

A RETIRED lawyer who has spent most of his life out of the public eye gave the Universities Endowment Fund a $2 million boost yesterday.

The gift from Mr Koh Choon Joo, 96, better known among his friends and associates as C. J. Koh, is the largest single donation so far from an individual to set up a university professorship.

The money will set up the C.J. Koh Professorship in Law at the National University of Singapore (NUS).

As he is in poor health, he was unable to attend yesterday's cheque-presentation ceremony at the Shangri-La Hotel.

His friend and trustee, Mr Ong Tiong Tat, 57, presented the cheque to Professor Lim Pin, vice-chancellor of the NUS, and Professor Arthur Lim, chairman of the endowment fund's fund-raising committee.

The Government will match the donation dollar for dollar.

Yesterday's ceremony was attended by Chief Justice Yong Pung How, Education Minister Lee Yock Suan, academics and members of the fund's board of advisers and fund-raising committee.

Fundraiser Susie Tan, 40, who played a key role in bringing together Mr Koh and the university fund, described him as a self-made man whose wealth was a result of many years of hard work and prudent investment.

"Money was not everything to him, enough was enough," said Ms Tan, the vice-president and group head (legal and secretariat) of Sembawang Corporation.

In a letter of thanks to Mr Koh, President Ong Teng Cheong, who is patron-in-chief of the fund, said: "I

■ See also: Page 40

am sure this gesture will encourage others who have the means to make similar donations to the universities.

"Such gifts will not only perpetuate their names and their generosity but also help in the education of young Singaporeans so that they can serve the country."

Professor Lim Pin said: "Very rarely do we get money paid in one lump sum at the very beginning.

"With most professorships, the money is pledged over several years. As a result, in many of the past professorships, the money has not been collected fully."

He said that aside from Mr Koh's contribution, there was one other professorship for which the money was given in a lump sum.

This was the $2 million given by the Overseas Union Bank last year to set up a professorship in medicine at the NUS in the name of bank founder Lien Ying Chow.

Prof Lim said the university hoped to find a candidate for the C.J. Koh professorship in about six months' time

The candidate would be an authority in law who would lecture, teach, do research and may even be consulted by Government bodies or industry.

"We will try to make that person as widely useful as possible," he said.

The endowment fund, set up in 1991, is being reviewed to see how it can be improved and what targets should be set for the next five years.

Prof Arthur Lim said the target of $250 million could be raised in five years' time.

So far, more than $60 million has been raised.

He also said that he hoped someone else might take over his position as chairman of the fund's fund-raising committee in a year's time.

"It's always the same face when it comes to appeals," he said. "There are advantages to having a new face."

Bernard Leong

Universities become great not because of the great infrastructure but the graduates they produce.

If you examine the history of Singapore in the past century, we can find local philanthropists such as Lee Kong Chian and Tan Kah Kee, who have donated portions of their wealth to building schools and funding scholarships (I happen to one of the lucky recipients from the Lee Foundation for my PhD studies) and it does not mean that we can sit back and wait for those who have the money to do it. We can contribute back to society by effort. In fact, we can offer just as much by this form of giving. We can bring about small changes that can help to make the daily lives of others better. Here is how I see it: if five out of 10 of my friends are doing something to help make society better, we are inspiring another five idealistic, passionate and aspiring people who will create virtuous cycles for many of the future generations.

I have often conceived giving back to NUS in the form of effort, by educating the future generation and hopefully they will be spurred to great heights.

I often emphasised to the students I have taught that it is important to give back to the university. One important lesson I have learnt from my experiences abroad is that many universities become great not because of the great infrastructure but the graduates they produce.

Wong Tien Yin

Prof Wong is currently Professor and Director of the Singapore Eye Research Institute, National University of Singapore. He holds a concurrent Professorship at the University of Melbourne. He is the Principal Investigator of multi-centred projects in Australia, the US and Singapore, and has been awarded more than $20 million in peer-reviewed grant funding. For his research and philanthropy, he was named one of the Ten Outstanding Young Persons of the World for "academic leadership in people younger than 40 years of age" (1999) and he received the Asia Pacific Academy of Ophthalmology Prevention of Blindness (2003) and Distinguished Service (2005) Award.

Poh Soo Chuan

Poh Soo Chuan is Senior Physician and Associate Professor of Medicine, National University of Singapore who gives thousands of dollars each year to support medical education with no fanfare. He is an important silent giver.

Gerard Ee

Gerard Ee started his career as an accountant in 1974. He became a practising auditor in 1976 and retired as a partner of Ernst & Young on 30 June 2005.

Mr Ee has been active in the field of social service throughout his professional life as an accountant. He helped convert a programme providing respite care into the Assisi Home and Hospice in 1987 and was its Chairman until 2002. In 1989 he established Bizlink Centre, an employment programme for the disabled, and was its Chairman until 1992. He has chaired a whole range of social service organisations and programmes which include juvenile rehabilitative centres, grassroots organisations, schools, and various programmes for the elderly and youth. He was also an active member of the Task Force which established the Code on Religious Harmony.

Mr Ee was officially appointed as Chairman of the National Kidney Foundation on 17 July 2005.

Lions SaveSight Centre (Singapore)

Diabetes Kills, Cripples And Blinds

Lion International formed Singapore SaveSight Centre to address this problem.

Big names weigh in to fight diabetes scourge

Affected by the disease too, they want to use their clout to raise awareness of the illness

By Salma Khalik
Health Correspondent

EYE surgeon Arthur Lim, lawyer Harry Elias and the Reverend James Wong have one thing in common — they are all diabetic or on the verge of becoming so, and want to use their clout to raise awareness of the illness here.

These friends got fired up late last year, following reports that diabetes was fast becoming Asia's major killer. Singapore itself logs one of the world's highest rates of the disease, marked by the body's inability to control the level of sugar in the blood.

Professor Lim, 71, calls it an epidemic that is going to get worse. Together with another eight to 10 friends in positions of power or influence, the trio want to help beat the scourge which leads to amputations, blindness, loss of kidney function, heart attacks, strokes and death.

They believe it is cheaper to prevent the illness than to see a good part of the health budget blown to manage it after its onset.

Health Minister Khaw Boon Wan, when told about the plan for the public education drive, said: "Wonderful! We need many more such civic groups."

Prof Lim's group also hopes to work with the Diabetes Society in its mission, an invitation which was welcomed last week by society chairman Warren Lee.

It is tie-ups like this which will help Prof Lim make his group "a very strong organisation".

Veteran lawyer Mr Elias, calling this "no idl boast", wants a "blitzkrieg" — akin to the lightning war that the Germans used so well in Worl War II — against the illness.

The group wants to educate not just patient but also clinic nurses and general practitione (GPs), after having found out that only a third GPs check their diabetic patients' feet.

Associate Professor Goh Lee Gan, the vi president of the College of Family Physicia conceded that the level of care among GPs v ied, but that it was more important for patie to check their feet daily and see a doctor if th are sores or redness.

For diabetics, untreated ulcers and even nor cuts on their feet can lead to gangrene amputations. Diabetics here lost 500 legs t knife last year. Almost nine in 10 of such a tations were needless.

Diabetic retinopathy, the leading cau blindness, is also preventable with early ment, said Prof Lim, the former head of th gapore National Eye Centre. An even l concern is that half the 330,000 diabetic are now unaware they have the disease, a other half a million will develop it.

Mr Elias said: "Diabetes cannot be cur it can be controlled. But how can you con you don't even know you have it?"

NEED TO FIND OUT

"Diabetes cannot be cured, but it can be controlled. But how can you control it if you don't even know you have it?"

LAWYER HARRY ELIAS (right)

IT CAN BE DONE

"All we need is 1,000 people donating $1,000 each to get $1 million. I'm a good beggar."

EYE SURGEON ARTHUR LIM (left), who is confident funding will not be a problem

Rev Wong, 67, is certain the group can make a mark.

"Everything has to start small," said the pastor of St Andrew's Cathedral. Unlike his two friends, he is not diabetic, but on the verge of becoming so. Since he found out his condition more than a year ago, he has been careful about his diet. He said he will not "directly preach" about diabetes, but will encourage people to eat better and exercise regularly.

The group will also get the help of lawyer Pathmanaban Selvadurai, 73. Diabetic since 1989, he has learnt how to keep his blood sugar level under control.

Launching the campaign will take money.

Said Prof Lim, who has raised hundreds of millions of dollars for the National University of Singapore: "All we need is 1,000 people donating $1,000 each to get $1 million. I'm a good beggar."

salma@sph.com.sg

Diabetics at risk of blindness

The risk is serious but simple eye screening and early detection can make a big difference,

In Singapore about 10 per cent of those over 40 years are effected by diabetes – one of the highest rates in the developed world.

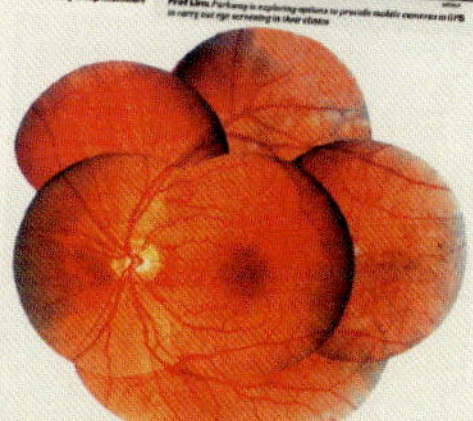

Proliferative diabetic retinopathy

A group of well intentioned individuals decided to join forces to create awareness and combat this dreadful disease that is crippling some 300,000 Singaporeans. Societies and charitable groups such as the Diabetes Society play an important role to raise public awareness.

"Wonderful! We need many more such civic groups,"

Health Minister Khaw Boon Wan

Singapore Lions Celebrate 50 Years of Giving in Singapore

THE STRAITS TIMES FRIDAY, OCTOBER 17 2008

1958 50 2008

Singapore Lions Clubs

Celebrating 50 years of Community Service

Prime Minister Lee Hsien Loong's Message

District Governor Bobby Eng's Message

WE SERVE

Lions Clubs International (LCI) is the world's largest service club organisation with 1.3 million members in approximately 45,000 clubs in 202 countries and geographical areas. Lions are men and women who volunteer their time to humanitarian causes. Founded in 1917, the volunteer organisation's motto is "We Serve". Since then, the association of Lions clubs has provided millions of people with the opportunity to give something back to their communities. In July 2007, Financial Times published a rating of worldwide NGOs and Lions Clubs International was ranked the best to work with. Lions in Singapore have been volunteering their time and efforts to serving the local community since 1958, with membership of over 1700 members in 71 clubs.

Lions SaveSight Centre (Singapore) emerges

Arthur Lim with Guest of Honour SM Goh Chok Tong and President, Peter Lim

District Governor Bobby Eng (left), President Peter Lim (centre) with Honorary Lion Professor Donald Tan

The Silent GIVERS

" Let me give you a specific example of how one couple who has done well in life is giving something back to society. The couple prefers to remain anonymous. With their encouragement, our CCMC has started a new Youth Development Programme this year to help academically weak students from poor families to do better. The objectives are to instil confidence in these students and help them to do well in school. These students will have to attend tuition classes twice a week in the afternoon. The programme started in March this year with 20 students from Primary 4 to Primary 6.

The couple has donated $30,000 for the upgrade of computers and pledged $30,000 per year for recurrent expenditure for a minimum period of five years. In total, they have committed $180,000 to this programme, a generous sum indeed. They will review the results at the end of five years. If they are satisfied that the programme is effective, they will continue to support it. This is a fine example of head, heart and hands in action."

Excerpt of speech by SM Goh Chok Tong,
Marine Parade National Day Dinner,
16 August 2008

Mrs Arthur Lim

For many years, Mrs Arthur Lim joined her husband in numerous trips throughout Asia when Arthur was demonstrating live surgery, lecturing, advising and discussing with national leaders regarding how the eye surgeons of each nation can contribute.

Mrs Lim seen here in Bangladesh with Prof Martin, Minister for Health of Bangladesh and other Bangladeshi eye surgeons.

Charity Wai

Charity is another silent giver, dedicated to the development of medicine and ophthalmology. It can be said that she is the key person behind the development of SNEC, one of the world's most important global eye centres. She spent much time with Arthur Lim in his international developments and contributed significantly to the success of the 26th World Congress of Ophthalmology in 1990 when she was the General Manager of the congress.

Doris Poh

Mrs Poh is another silent giver quietly helping others – tackling relatively small problems of ordinary people like gardeners, factory workers, maids, etc. Maybe it is a reflection of her training as a social worker. She is the wife of Dr Poh Soo Chuan.

Julie Yeong

Julie worked for over 25 years with Arthur Lim putting numerous important manuscripts and international decisions into nicely presented documents. In particular, Julie helped in the production of over 30 books written by Arthur. The most well-known is the Colour Atlas of Ophthalmology, published in nine languages, which has sold over 50,000 copies.

Chiam Soo Lee

Chiam Soo Lee spent 25 years as Personal Assistant and General Manager running organisations led by Arthur Lim who moves rapidly from meetings to meetings in different countries. For years, she helped to put together the numerous proposals he was involved in.

She is seen here at the Great Hall of China when the Chinese government recognised Arthur Lim's significant contributions to the People's Republic of China.

CHAPTER 6

Medical Alumni GIVES

The Medical Alumni is a place for graduates of the medical profession to gather. Doctors were joined by dentists and pharmacists and more recently graduate nurses. The most important function of the Medical Alumni and its activities is to gel the medical profession together in informal gatherings.

My opinion is that the Alumni's function is to bond everyone together. This is an extraordinary and unique role. It is a marketplace for colleagues and friends to shop for ideas, to air grievances and to discover what has gone wrong with our health services.

Where members and their friends meet in our informal, friendly and relaxed atmosphere, where students and young doctors talk as equals with their deans and consultants. Where the Vice-Chancellor, permanent secretaries or the director of medical services, do not pull ranks and will sit with ordinary doctors, dental surgeons and pharmacists, to discuss each other's problems. Such a setting creates a bond for everyone.

(From the 75 Years of Our Alumni)

Agong Gives by Persuasion – sometimes scolding

Chee Phui Hung, Agong, ruled the Medical Alumni for 50 years and created the success and bonds among members of the medical profession. He is now 86 and at recent meetings, he agreed that there should be a successor and created the term "King Arthur".

The bond of Alumni leaders

Five National Leaders were Guests of Honour at the Alumni Association's Events

Two stimuli that attract support for the Alumni Association are the visits by social, political leaders and their bonding with NUS.

1995 Annual Dinner

Dr Mahathir Bin Mohamad

Dr Mahathir meets the US Ambassador, Timothy Choba

Hasmah (Dr Mahathir's wife) dancing with classmate, Arthur.

1998 Annual Dinner

Dr Tony Tan

Dr Tony Tan meets new Honorary Member, Tan Sri Dato Dr Abu Bakar Suleiman, Director General of Health, Malaysia.

President Nathan with medical graduates and the famous Dr Lim Hock Siew.

2001 Annual Dinner

President S R Nathan

SM Goh Chok Tong becomes Hononrary member of Medical Alumni.

2004 Annual Dinner

SM Goh Chok Tong

2007 Annual Dinner

Mr Khaw Boon Wan

Health Minister Khaw Boon Wan persuading doctors to work together for greater progress.

DOCTORS ARE The Silent GIVERS

What Makes Me Give?
Dr Wong Sze Tai

During my training as a Child and Adolescent Psychiatrist, I was made to observe very young children. One thing which struck me was that when a baby sees another child crying, the baby would crawl to this crying child, give something to the child and look intently at the child as if to tell the child, "Don't cry. I have this for you." This is the beginning of giving to others which is evident even from babyhood. Unfortunately, as the baby grows up, people may teach him to be selfish and he will lose his innate tendency to be kind towards his fellow human beings.

Why don't we nurture the child and help him to preserve his kindness instead of killing it?

I was so impressed with the thought that it stuck in my mind and I wanted to translate this into my work.

The story that I am sharing is based on my own experience. Doctors donate individually to many charities. Doctors who do not charge patients who cannot afford to pay are also performing a charitable act. Being a humane doctor is to be able to comfort and reassure those who are suffering, and this includes sharing their pain and sorrow. Giving my patients hope and seeing them leave my consultation room with hope in their hearts is what I strive for as a doctor.

I teach my medical students and doctors this very important principle – what you learn, you must also give back to society. You can also give your time. One example I have is the case of a Secondary Two girl who refused to go to school for two years. To help her to go back to school, I had to gain her trust. I did this by driving her to school every morning as part of the treatment to help her confront her fears. What her parents and teachers could not accomplish, I managed to do as a doctor. I think no other Child and Adolescent Psychiatrist will do something like this. For six months, I would get up at 5am on schooldays to drive to her home, then send her to school at 6am, at no charge. She got a free ride to school in comfort. On arrival, she would be handed over to the Principal and Vice-Principal who were there to welcome her every day. The Principal and Vice-Principal spent a lot of time with me discussing how to help the girl to return to school, as they did not know how to handle the situation.

In the end, the girl was able to integrate into the class and she was able to progress to Secondary Three and Four. I followed up with her when she went to Junior College. There were times when she would relapse and I would repeat the same treatment, but this did not happen for more than six months at a stretch. She passed her "A" levels with good results and went to Canada to pursue her studies. She now aspires to be a doctor.

This is my way of giving back as a humane and caring doctor.

The other story is about a girl who had refused to go to school for the past four years since Primary Two. Her mother suffered from depression and she kept her child at home as she needed her company. When the girl saw me, she had very low self-esteem.

Her mother is my patient. She is separated from her husband. She came to consult me as a patient suffering from depression and her daughter would accompany her each time she came to the clinic.

Then I got to know about her daughter's problem. The only way she would communicate with me was by writing. I would write what I wanted to enquire from her and she would respond. By doing this, each session would last two hours or more. As they were relatively poor, quite often I would not charge them. If the patient insisted on paying, I would charge them between $20 to $30 as a token.

The girl subsequently passed her PSLE with distinctions. She went to secondary school where she had a relapse and was given the same treatment regime. She passed her "O" levels and was one of the best students in school. The same thing happened in Junior College. She got into university and kept in contact and I continued to see her. During her university days, she was exempted from presenting projects because of her condition. She did very well in her exams.

As part of giving back to my alma mater and fellow colleagues and friends, I devote myself to helping out at the Alumni Association. I was Chairman from 1989 onwards. What I have learnt is whatever we do to help our fellowmen, we should do it with commitment and dedication, without asking for kudos, favours or praise. The important thing is you must want to help out. This is a way of giving back to society.

President, Medical Alumni of Malaysia Gives

Mr Tong Yew Sum

Mr Tong Yew Sum recently retired as Executive Director of Apex Pharmacy Corporate Sdn. Bhd., a subsidiary of APEX HEALTHCARE BHD., a vertically intergated pharmaceutical healthcare company listed on the First Board of Bursa Malaysia. Mr Tong was President of the Alumni Association (2006–2007) and the Past President of the Malaysian Organisation of Pharmaceutical Industries (MOPI). His interests include golf (the game and assembling of golf clubs), bird watching and photography.

In Giving, We Sing, Dance and Have Fun

Jeffrey Seow, William Chew, Arthur Lim, Peter Tay and Loh Hong Sai.

Roy Ang

George Wong and wife Jennifer Foo

Singing doctors: Wong Kai Peng and William Tseng

Freda with magician, George Wong

Friendship, Bonds, Informal Gatherings of Medical Graduates in Malaysia (Kuala Lumpur) and Singapore

Graduates include Chan Beng Keat, Paul Ngui, Loke Kwok Kheong, A Canaganayagam and Mahmood Merican

Agong with Health Minister Khaw Boon Wan and students.

Puvan Singh "belly dancing" with Chao Tzee Cheng.

Alumni and VIPs

Director of Medical Services, Dr K Satku, met leading medical alumni members from Malaysia – Tan Sri Dato Dr Haji Abdul Majid B Ismail and Dr Loke Kwok Kheong.

SM Goh Chok Tong met the Alumni officials and Shih Choon Fong.

CHAPTER 7

NUS Students in Cambodia

NUS Students in Cambodia

"Why help the poor in Cambodia when there are so many needy people in Singapore?"

My friend posed the question to me before I embarked on my first trip to Cambodia. I was taken aback at first, as I had never thought of it before, therefore I was caught unawares. I tried to convince him about the dire conditions in Cambodia and how we could help them. Nevertheless, the question remained, and to a certain extent I did agree with him. I told him that I would keep it at the back of my mind during the trip, and hopefully I would be able to find some answers there.

And so, with purposeful hearts and a load full of eagerness, 21 medical students, four dental students and five doctors embarked on the 3rd Project Lokun trip to Cambodia. Our mission: To provide sustainable healthcare and health education to the villages in the Pursat region.

The first sight that greets you at the villages is those of filth and poverty. The stench that fills the air would wake you up from any coma. Children can be seen running about barefooted, clothed in disgustingly smelly and tattered attire, their every movement tracked by swarms of flies. Yet, amidst all their poverty, their greeting smiles warmed our hearts, and bridged the air of alienisms.

My experience at the floating village of Kampong Luon was indeed an eye-opener. The complexity of their Kampong thoroughly fascinated me. There were houses-cum-shops that sold daily necessities and cooked food, barbers and even a diesel kiosk. The Kampong was also well dissected into major and minor waterways, clearly demonstrating some form of urban planning. Thankfully, we had our trustworthy boatman who knew the Kampong inside-out, as a lack of street signs would definitely leave us stranded in the biggest lake in South-East Asia. Another sight to behold was that of the many sampans tugging floating homes towards the shore. Subsequently, I found out that they migrate in response to the changes in seasonal water levels. We were warmly welcomed by the locals with melodious songs and great applause. This injected a steroid of enthusiasm into the running of the clinics. Throughout our four days of clinics, we provided consultation and symptomatic treatment to nearly 500 people in the region of Pursat.

In addition to running clinics, we also educated the villages on topics such as hygiene and sanitation, dental care, and dietary lifestyle. We were very encouraged by their receptiveness and intelligence.

Wound debridement

House-to-house education

Handwashing in schools

The mainstay of our education programme was that of school education. Throughout four days of school education, we interacted with 600 children, ranging from seven to 11 years of age. The syllabus was taught to the children in a fun and engaging manner, through the use of appealling visual aids, skits, games and freebies. Seeing the happy and enthusiastic faces of these children provided us with great joy and satisfaction. It was a heart-rending experience each time we had to leave the company of these adorable school children. However, we know that we would see them again in the next trip.

I fondly remember an occasion when we were putting up a health education skit for a group of adolescents. At the end of the day, they volunteered to re-enact the skit, adding more humour and realism to our original script. Most importantly, they kept reminding one another of the hygiene practices we educated them on. Through this incident, I began to comprehend that we had the power to influence the lives of the youths, inculcating good health practices and values in them. And with their youthful exuberance, they would spread our messages to many others, and allowing many to benefit from them.

In many community projects, participants would leave feeling a sense of achievement having built a school or dug a well. Unfortunately, we left the villages feeling more helpless and dejected. We felt extremely inadequate in dealing with the chronic problems that plague the poor in Cambodia. We were left baffled by the dire state of the government hospitals, the inappropriately priced medications for the poor and the countless obstacles we encountered from their government just so that we could provide aid.

We believe that the key to the sustainability and success

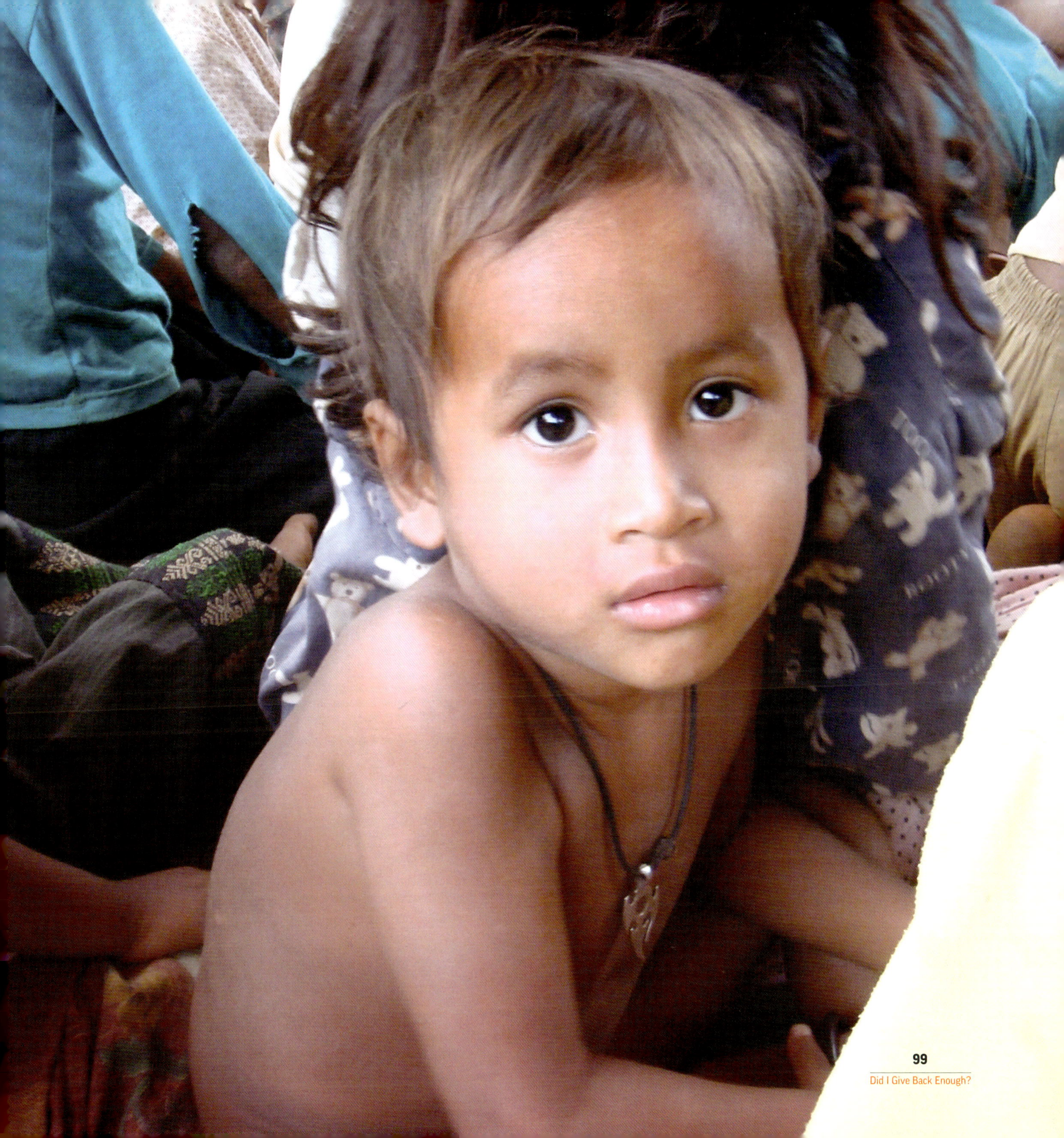

of our project would be that of primary prevention and a good referral system for chronic illnesses. As such we would place great emphasis on developing and improving our health education materials and syllabus. In addition, we intend to fine-tune our referral programme for chronic illnesses, to make in sustainable in our absence.

Our project has taken one small step in helping the Cambodians. However, many more leaps are required to improve the lives of the needy in Cambodia. The long-term success of this project though, will depend on continued support from our community. We desperately require new blood, passionate people who can inject fresh ideas, and most importantly, leaders to spearhead the project in the near future.

And finally, after three trips to Cambodia with Project Lokun, I have found my response to the conundrum: I know that there will always be needy people, locally and abroad, who require our help. But after this trip, I have come to realise that the most precious gift is that of sacrifice, a sacrifice of love, time and effort. The surrender of one's self for the cause.

I have found my cause, to devote myself to the needy in Cambodia. Have you?

Medical Students Bring Health Screening To The Heartlanders

What can Medical students do for the community?

As medical students, we pledge to learn the art of doctoring so as to serve mankind and our community in the future. However, in this early phase of our training, our skills and knowledge are still grossly limited. We cannot write medical certificate for our patients. We cannot diagnose diseases confidently. And most certainly, we cannot prescribe medications to alleviate the suffering of the patients.

So, is there anything Medical students can do for the community?

Public Health Screening (PHS) is a free mass health screening exercise for members of the public that the NUS Medical Society organises every year.

The event aims to help those who are not regularly checked by a doctor. Any common diseases they may be suffering from in their early stages can be detected and they can seek medical help before these diseases cause irreversible harm to the body. Held at prominent public areas, PHS also strives to raise health awareness in the general public.

Members of the public who participate in PHS will answer brief questions regarding their health screening habits and their general health, have their body mass index, blood pressure and capillary blood sugar measured and then finally have a doctor or senior medical student explain to them the findings of the screening. They will also receive a goodie bag filled with health messages in the form of fruits, juices and pamphlets.

Working together with newly graduated students and senior doctors, students from all levels come together to perform this free service for the community. One can feel the enthusiasm surging through the entire arena and imagine the possibilities when the entire faculty and profession come together as one united entity.

It is no wonder that PHS has yielded fantastic response over the past few years. Weeks before the event, before any publicity material has been sent out, people will start writing in to ask "when is the next PHS?" The number of people screened has steadily increased from 1,200 in 2006 to more than 2,100 in 2007.

Over the years, the methods used for screening have also

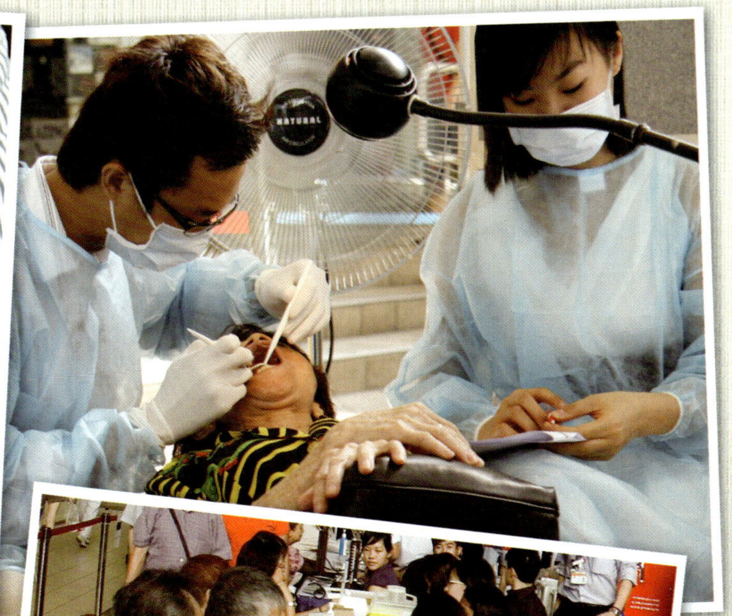

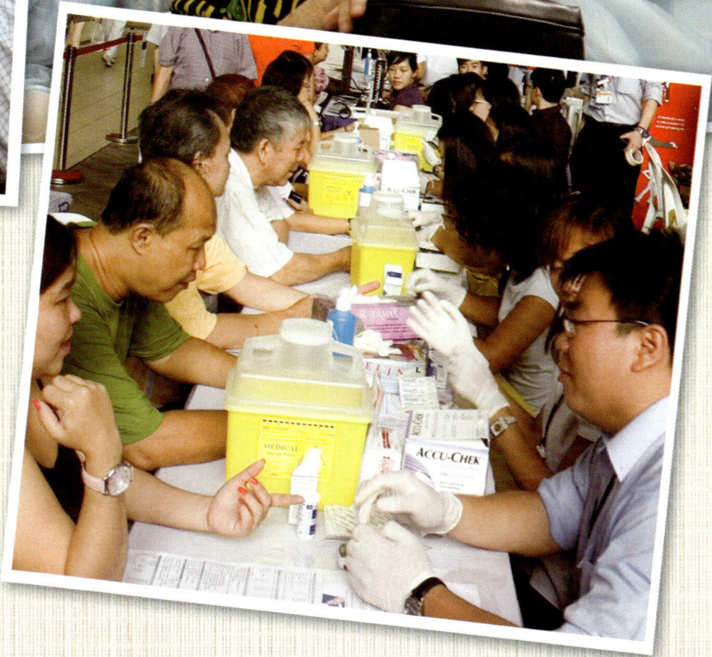

been refined with rigourous research in scientific literature. Collaborating with the polyclinics, we will be able provide more comprehensive services to the people we screen.

The Neighbourhood Health Screening (NHS) is yet another project initiated, organised and run by medical students. Health screening is performed door-to-door in rental flats that house needy residents who often shun away from health screening due to poor access to health services or even the fear of discovering diseases they are suffering from. This format ensures that the service is provided to those who would otherwise be missed if the screening was performed at the void decks or other public areas.

We are hence able to identify and refer residents with social and financial troubles to the grassroots organisations who are able to extend their helping hand to them.

All these go one full circle when the students learn from participating in such activities. Whether it is giving advice to curb blood pressure control in hypertensive patients, or taking the capillary blood glucose reading for a man with suspected diabetes, we learn from the people we serve. It is our privilege that residents willingly open doors not only to their homes but also to their lives for us.

So, I ask again, is there anything Medical students can do for the community?

I will answer that question with an emphatic "YES!" And there is so much more that can be done.

BONDS

Bonds of students with graduates

Students build friendships and bond with Director of Medical Services, Dr K Satku, and leaders of the medical alumni.

CHAPTER 8

A World Class Eye Centre in Tianjin, China

Tianjin Medical University Eye Centre

On 29 September 1989, the International Intraocular Implant Training Centre (IIITC) was officially opened.

It was Prof Arthur Lim who initiated and suggested raising funds from all over the world to set up such a centre in Tianjin Medical College and its affiliates in adjoining rural areas. His suggestion was met with enthusiastic responses and warm support from international ophthalmologists, and the approval of the State Council and the Municipal Government of Tianjin was obtained. It is the first centre in the world to be built exclusively for extracapsular cataract extraction (ECCE) and posterior chamber implant (PCI) surgery, and operates with the primary objective that: "If you give a man a fish, you can feed him for a day. But if you teach him how to fish, he can feed himself for a lifetime."

Sixteen-Year Developments

Since September 1989 to 2005, the Centre has conducted 47 week-long training courses, some of which were conducted within the Centre and some were conducted outside. A total of 2,648 ophthalmologists have been trained.

More than 230 ophthalmologists from all over China, including Tibet and Taiwan, were attached to the Centre for a three-month or a half-year intensive training course. They worked as assistant residents, attending outpatient clinics, looking after patients in the wards, assisting surgery and performing wet lab surgeries.

Besides domestic doctors, the Centre also received foreign ophthalmologists as students. Dr Mau Imo from Samoa was the first foreign ophthalmologist to take on a 10-month attachment in the Centre, from September 1997 to July 1998.

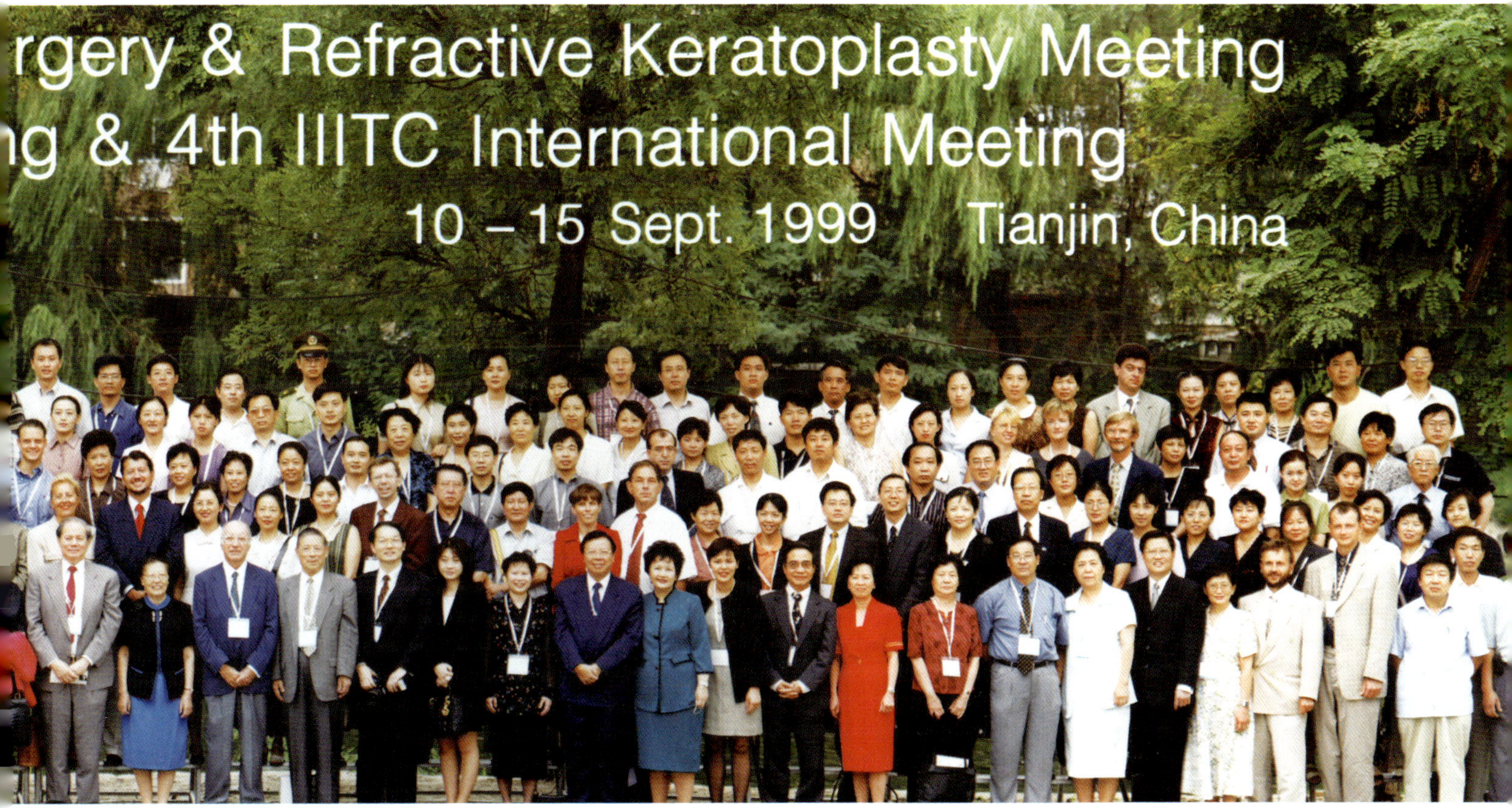

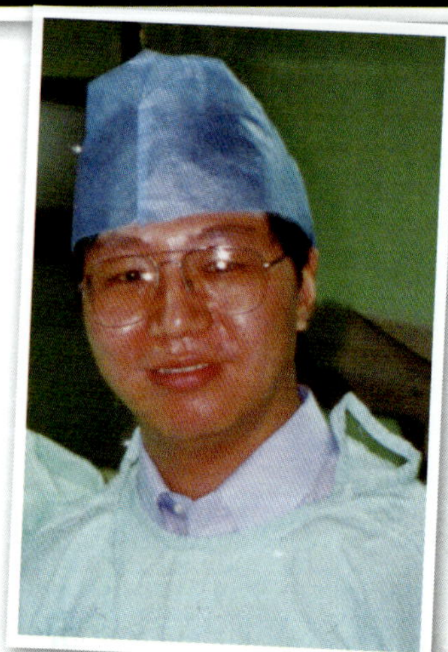

Li Xiao Rong, Medical Director of Tianjin Eye Centre

Tianjin Eye Centre was successful not just because of the excellent infrastrature but more importantly the commitment by local and foreign eye surgeons who selflessly helped to develop the centre.

Because of the training, she mastered the technique of microsurgery and implant surgery and became one of only two eye doctors in Samoa. Dr Tilahun Kiros Meshesha from Ethiopia came to the Centre in 1999. He completed his Master's degree in May 2002. And in September 2002, Dr Syed Wajahat Hassan from Pakistan was on an attachment for several months at the Centre.

The Centre has set up nearly 30 affiliated hospitals in different parts of China and sent doctors to develop implant surgery in 101 hospitals of 22 provinces.

After 16 years, the Centre and its all affiliated hospitals have carried out total of 650,000 implant surgeries.

Yuan – a Remarkable Leader of China

"Once in many decades, an ophthalmologist stands out above everyone else to change problems into opportunities. Professor Yuan Jia-Qin has inspired ophthalmic progress in China and the world."

Arthur Lim

Phase II Expansion

Growing from strength to strength, IIITC ventured from a mere cataract and implant centre to other fields in ophthalmology. By 1996, the number of cases treated at the Centre expanded to include corneal diseases, glaucoma, trauma and diabetic retinopathy besides cataract. The original site was just too small. Thus, the Centre had to be expanded into a comprehensive institution of many departments. The initial proposal was agreed upon and supported by Prof Arthur Lim and his family. Prof Lim and his family, including many of their friends donated generously again to the Centre. In addition, it was strongly supported by the Tianjin Municipal Government. The Phase II expansion project was completed on the 10th Anniversary of the Centre in 1999. The occasion also marked its transformation from the International Intraocular Implant Training Centre (IIITC) to the Tianjin Medical University Eye Centre (TMUEC).

Transformation from IIITC to TMUEC

Over the past 16 years, the Centre has completely become a comprehensive Eye Centre. At present, the Centre has evolved and matured with the establishment of five subspecialties: Cataract. Vitreo Retina, Cornea and Refractive surgery, Glaucoma and laser treatment for eye diseases. We also have Paediatric Ophthalmology, Aesthetic Eyelastic and Eye trauma. The Centre is capable of performing the following operations or giving treatment for the following diseases: cataract operation by using different methods with IOL implantation including clear cornea or sclera tunnel phacoemulsification, extracapsular cataract extraction, none phaco none suture self-sealing sclera tunnel incision, and etc, retinal detachment, vitrectomy and laser therapy for diabetic retinopathy, glaucoma, and refractive surgery using Excimer Laser. The patients ranged in age from several months to more than 100 years old, all with successful results after surgery.

SightFirst China Action

This initiative was a cooperative effort of China and Lions Clubs International. The Tianjin Medical University Eye Centre has been actively involved in the SightFirst China Action campaign from the very beginning. From 1997 to 2004, the Centre had sent out six national teams, with regard to this campaign, to various locations including the mountainous areas in middle China, Inner Mongolia, Southwest and Northwest China and the impoverished areas. A total of 2,537 cases of implant surgery had been accomplished altogether.

Working in a national SightFirst China Action team for the eradication of cataract blindness, all the teams showed dedication and perseverance. The teams were usually overloaded with duties and suffered from altitude sickness, colds and gastro-intestinal troubles. But they never complained or stopped working, because they knew that they not only gave sight to a cured patient himself, the entire family also benefit from it. It was this tremendous sense of duty and honours in their work that kept members of the national teams working so hard.

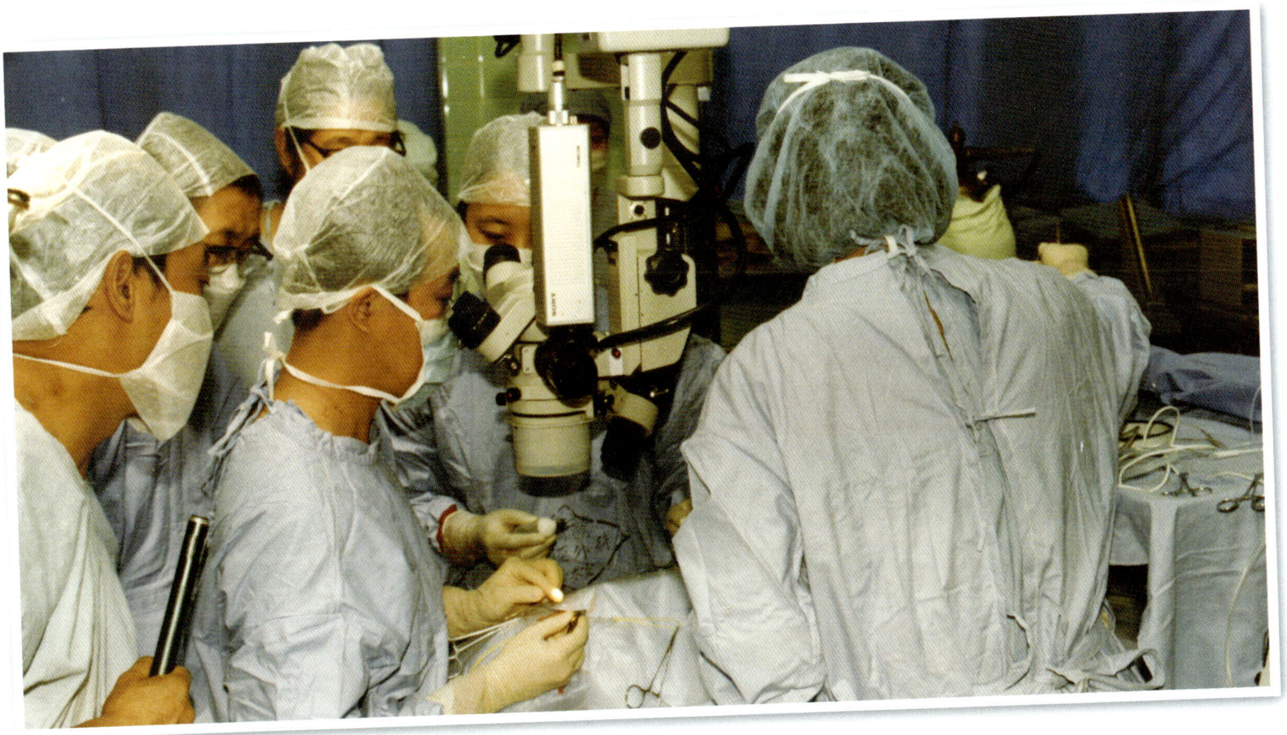

Ang Beng Chong, a superb teacher and surgeon, performing live surgery demonstration in China.

"The ICO expresses its great appreciation and deepest admiration for your contribution to ophthalmic education and patient care worldwide. ... Your leadership in establishing the Singapore National Eye Centre as one of the great eye centers of the world... your support of eye centres and eye surgery in China and all of Asia... is a great contribution to the elevation of ophthalmic education and eyecare throughout the world."

International Council of Ophthalmology

International Council of Ophthalmology

CONCILIUM OPHTHALMALOGICUM UNIVERSALE

A Special Tribute to

Professor Arthur S. M. Lim

March 2005

On behalf of World Ophthalmology, the International Council of Ophthalmology expresses its great appreciation and deepest admiration for your contributions to ophthalmic education and patient care worldwide. Your distinguished career of expert clinical service, innovative research and devotion to education is exemplary in the world ophthalmic community. Your leadership in establishing the Singapore National Eye Center as one of the great eye centers of the world, your hosting the XXVI International Congress of Ophthalmology in Singapore, your support of eye centers and eye surgery in China and all of Asia, and your numerous humanitarian efforts are a great contribution to the elevation of ophthalmic education and eyecare throughout the world.

For Gottfried O.H. Naumann, President
Mark O.M. Tso, Vice-President
Bruce E. Spivey, Secretary-General
Balder Gloor, Treasurer
Members of International Council of Ophthalmology

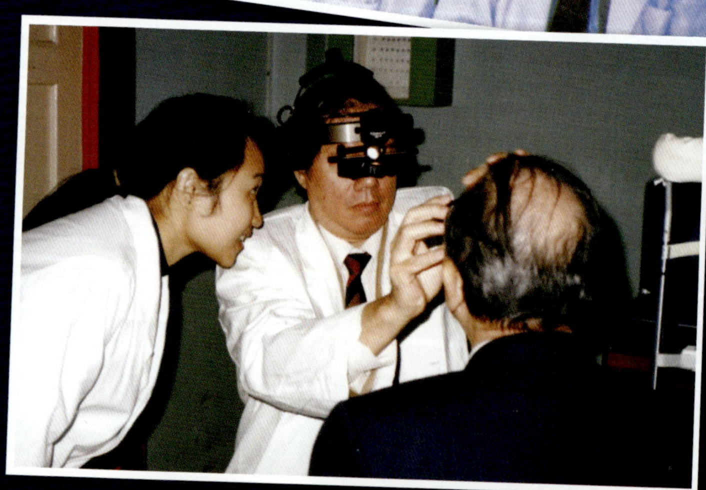

Meeting numerous officials in Tianjin including Vice-Premier Qian Qin-Chen

Recognition

Tianjin Medical University Eye Centre received an acclaimed title of being the "Founding Ground of the Demonstrations of Medical Science".

The success of Tianjin Medical University Eye Centre was given the most prestigious recognition in its history in May 2002 when it was awarded the top Science and Education model by the Chinese Central Government on the recommendation of the All China Federation of Returned Overseas Chinese. Vice-Premier Qian Qi-Chen granted an interview to Prof Arthur Lim at the People's Great Hall in Beijing and congratulated him for the Centre's achievements.

Establishment of the College of Ophthalmology and Optometry, Tianjin Medical University

Twenty years ago, the School of Optometry was set up in Tianjin Medical University (TMU). In 2004, the President of TMU proposed that TMUEC be combined with the School of Optometry to organise a College of Ophthalmology and Optometry. In April of 2004, the College of Ophthalmology and Optometry, Tianjin Medical University was inaugurated. At present, we pay special attention to reform the School of Optometry to a higher standard. Meanwhile, we have set up close relations with Hong Kong Polytechnic University, the World Council of Optometry and the College of Optometry of Southern California in America. Prof Arthur Lim of Singapore

and Prof George Woo, the Chair Professor of the School of Optometry, Hong Kong Polytechnic University, have been appointed as the honorary Presidents of the College of Ophthalmology and Optometry, Tianjin Medical University. Other international cooperations are being discussed. Later on we will start to develop the School of Ophthalmology. We believe the College of Ophthalmology and Optometry, TMU will be the cradle of training ophthalmologists and optometrists in China.

International Exchange

Since the establishment of IIITC, the Centre invites well-known foreign experts to conduct lectures or demonstrate live surgeries every year. They come from Singapore, the United Belgium, Spain, India, Canada, Sweden, etc. Some of them have been invited to the Centre for two or more times.

Going abroad for international meetings is a major channel through which the Centre gains beneficial experiences and learns about the latest techniques. Not only does the Centre get to exchange experiences with foreign ophthalmologists but also develops and promotes friendship. Up to now, TMUEC has organised five international meetings in 1991, 1993, 1996, 1999 and 2003, all with great success. Following Prof Lim's suggestion, the Centre will organise its 6th international meeting – the 1st International Retina Meeting in Tianjin – in March, 2006.

"Arthur has single-handedly founded an ophthalmology centre in the medical college in Tianjin. No Singaporean who has served in China has done more than you have. No Singapore diplomat has been conferred the Medal of Friendship by the People's Republic of China as you have. No Singapore diplomat has been made honorary citizen of Tianjin and Xiamen as you have."

China honours Singaporean eye surgeon with top award

Recognition for helping to fight mass cataract blindness

By Mary Kwang
China Correspondent

BEIJING — Singaporean eye surgeon Professor Arthur Lim has won an international science and technology cooperation award from the Chinese government for helping to fight mass cataract blindness in that country.

The honour was given to Prof Lim by the State Science and Technology Commission (SSTC) for his contributions to ophthalmology technology. It was conferred alongside the country's most authoritative science and technology awards to local scientists.

A presentation ceremony was held at the Great Hall of the People on Friday for the scientists, officiated by President Jiang Zemin and attended by Premier Li Peng and Vice-Premiers Zhu Rongji and Li Lanqing.

Prof Lim, 63, who is the medical director of the Singapore National Eye Centre (SNEC), is one of two foreigners to win the honour this year.

The other winner is Mr Jean Pierre Lebrun of France for advancing Sino-European cooperation in the information field.

In a telephone interview, Prof Lim, who is in Singapore, said: "It's nice when Singapore, a small country, can work with a big country."

Giving credit to the people who work with him, he said: "It's teamwork. There are more than 10 eye doctors and administrative staff involved in the work."

Other awards

Prof Lim (left) has received other honours from China:

- Last year, he was given the Friendship Award by the Fujian government for his help in setting up the Xiamen Eye Centre.
- He has also been made an honorary citizen of Tianjin.

The award is only the latest honour heaped by China on Prof Lim, who has carried out ophthalmology work in that country for 12 years, including leading teams of eye surgeons to hold surgery demonstrations and setting up eye centres.

China has millions of cataract victims, but there are not enough trained ophthalmologists to perform cataract implant surgery.

Last year, Prof Lim was given the Friendship Award by the Fujian government for his help in setting up the Xiamen Eye Centre. He has also been made an honorary citizen of Tianjin.

The SNEC coordinates and liaises with eye centres in China that provide training in surgery to local ophthalmologists. It also helps in raising funds for such centres. Till date, Singapore has helped set up five eye centres in China.

Prof Lim, who founded the World Cataract Surgeons Society and has support from the World Bank, does similar work in India, Vietnam and Myanmar.

He is also looking into opening eye centres in Bangladesh.

Complimenting the Chinese for being good surgeons and quick learners, he remarked: "I think this has to do with the Chinese using chopsticks.

"That helps them control well the small muscles in the hand. The instruments for the eye are held like chopsticks."

Tommy Koh
Ambassador-At-Large, Ministry of Foreign Affairs

"This is a man who gives, a man who gives generously from his heart, unstingily and gives because of a sense of greater mission. This guy was mad to start the eye centre. Because in effect, he created and built up a whole generation of us, in the sense, even competing with his own practice, and again, it was typical of his generosity of spirit, to give so much more than what he was going to take out of the system.

So the result is now, 2004, he has at the rate of being immodest, I think, a great centre in Singapore, one which allows all of us to go round the world and hold our heads high as professionals, because we have been well trained, well exposed, but more importantly, as a doctor, the greatest honour you can have, is to sit at the feet of a master and see that you have learnt from him. So Arthur, on behalf of the entire generation of ophthalmologists in Singapore, thank you for everything you have done for us, in Singapore and the region and the world."

Vivian Balakrishnan
Minister for Community Development,
Youth and Sports and
2nd Minister for Information, Communications and the Arts

The Ten Eye Centres

Since 1989 Prof Arthur Lim has donated and raised funds to establish 10 eye centres in China for prevention of blindness. The first five eye Centres are Tianjin Medical University Eye Centre, Xiamen Eye Centre, Cataract Surgery Training Centre of Jinan, Shandong Province, Dept of Ophthalmology, NingXia People's Hospital and Dept of Ophthalmology, 2nd Affiliated Hospital of Lanzhou Medical College.

The next five eye Centres have been set up in succession from 2002. They are Dept of Ophthalmology in the Affiliated Hospital of Guiyang Medical College, Xingtai Eye Hospital, Zhou Kou Eye Hospital, the Dept of Ophthalmology in the 1st Affiliated Hospital of Kuming Medical College and the Dept of Ophthalmology in Sichuan People's Hospital.

These 10 centres have worked together with all of the eye surgeons for the eradication of cataract blindness in China and the blindness from cataract has been successfully controlled in China.

In Future

The Centre is now facing further expansion along with its rapid development, The current set-up is unable to meet the demands of increasing services. We plan to finish the Phase III expansion within five years. At the same time, we will develop the medical service on uveitis and oculoplasty, etc. Our target is to establish TMUEC as one of leading eye centres in China not only in medical service, education and training but also in academic research as well maintain its good reputation in the world.

The Centre is determined to do its utmost to fulfill the purpose for its existence, to introduce the most advanced techniques, and to promote the spirit of international friendship and cooperation; and to train highly-skilled ophthalmologists to restore eyesight to those who have lost it, to improve visual acuity to the people so they can adapt better to their work and life, and to bring happiness to humankind.

CHAPTER 9

GIVE TO THE POOREST

At the Missionary of Charities, Calcutta, India – Arthur meets Sister Nirmala (successor to Mother Theresa), to discuss giving help to the poorest of the poor.

To Me You're God

She was about fifty, a small plump woman with greying hair in a prim bun. Her daughter stood beside her holding her hand.

"Hello, Mrs Muthi," I greeted her. At once, she put out her other hand to find mine. I led her to a comfortable chair. "How are you after the flight?" I asked her when she sat down.

"It's very tiring. India is very far from Singapore!" she said with a laugh. "But my daughter and son came with me, so I am well taken care of."

"Good," I said, smiling at Miss Muthi. She nodded amiably at me.

"My mother is anxious to have the operation as soon as possible, doctor," Miss Muthi said.

"I know I'm being impatient, but I've been blind for four years and that is quite long enough,"Mrs Muthi said.

"I'm serious, Mrs Muthi," I said. "Would you tell me why you have chosen me to be your surgeon and travelled so far to come here?"

Mrs Muthi smiled shyly. "When my eye problems worsened, I spoke with the good doctors in New Dehli and Calcutta. I thought I would like to go overseas and get my eyes operated on. They gave me some names of European doctors and they also suggested you. I found out that you have written a book on cataracts. Of course, I couldn't read it with my eyes like this, but I read a review of it. I also heard from other doctors that you have taught in India and performed live operations. The professors I spoke to felt that I should come and see you. So although Singapore is far, I decided to come."

"Thank you for your confidence in me, Mrs Muthi," I said, pleased to know the reasons she has chosen me for her surgeon. "I've scheduled your operation for tomorrow morning," After we worked out some details, I said. "Mrs Muthi, you do know that you have other problems besides cataracts, so we cannot determine how much you can see after surgery."

"Only in statistics do people go blind by the millions. But each person goes blind by himself."

Sir John Wilson

Sir John Wilson - the world's most important leader and orator pushing thousands to help prevent blindness.

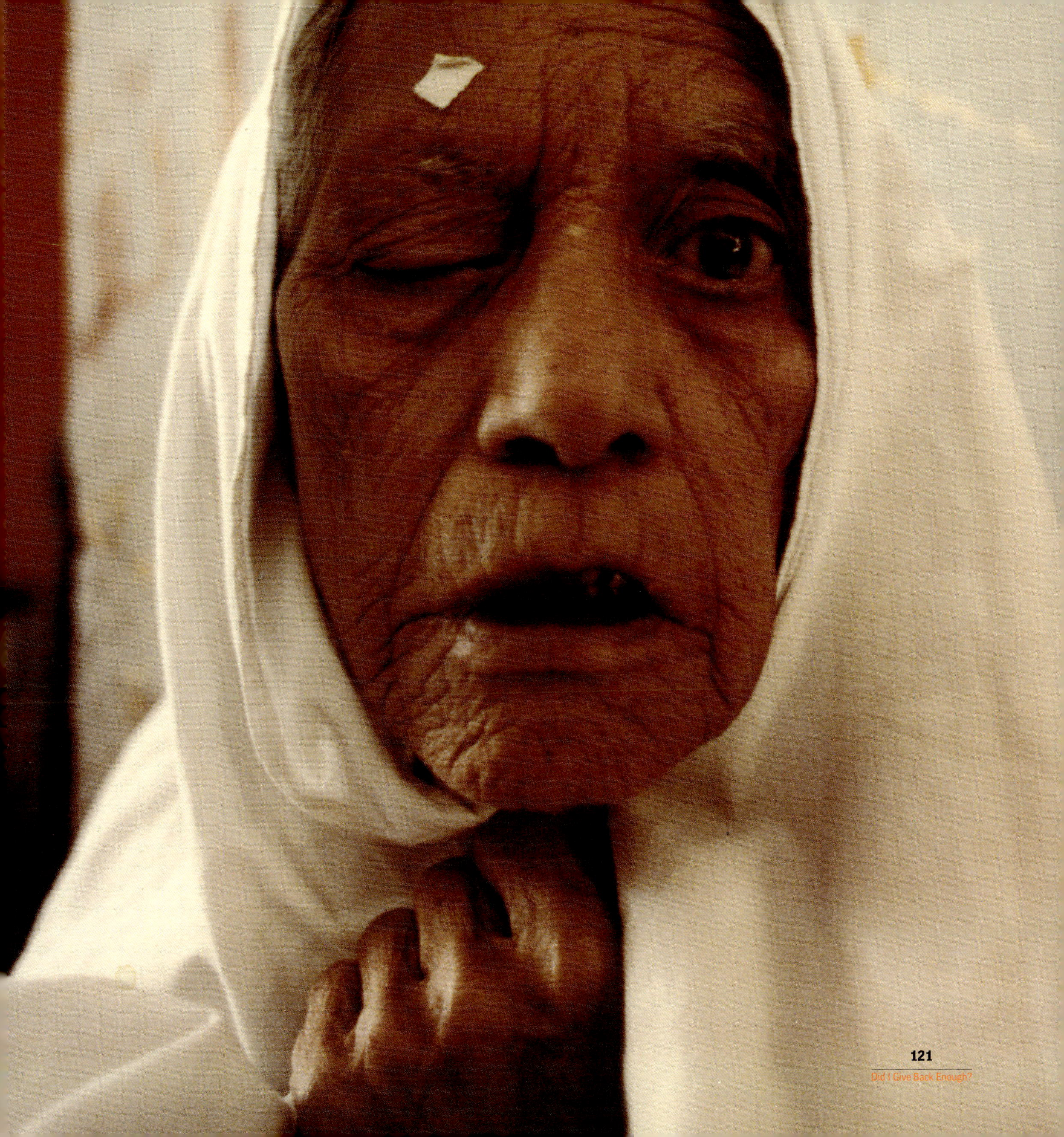

After Cataract Surgery in Bangladesh Eye Camp (One of the Poorest Countries in the World)

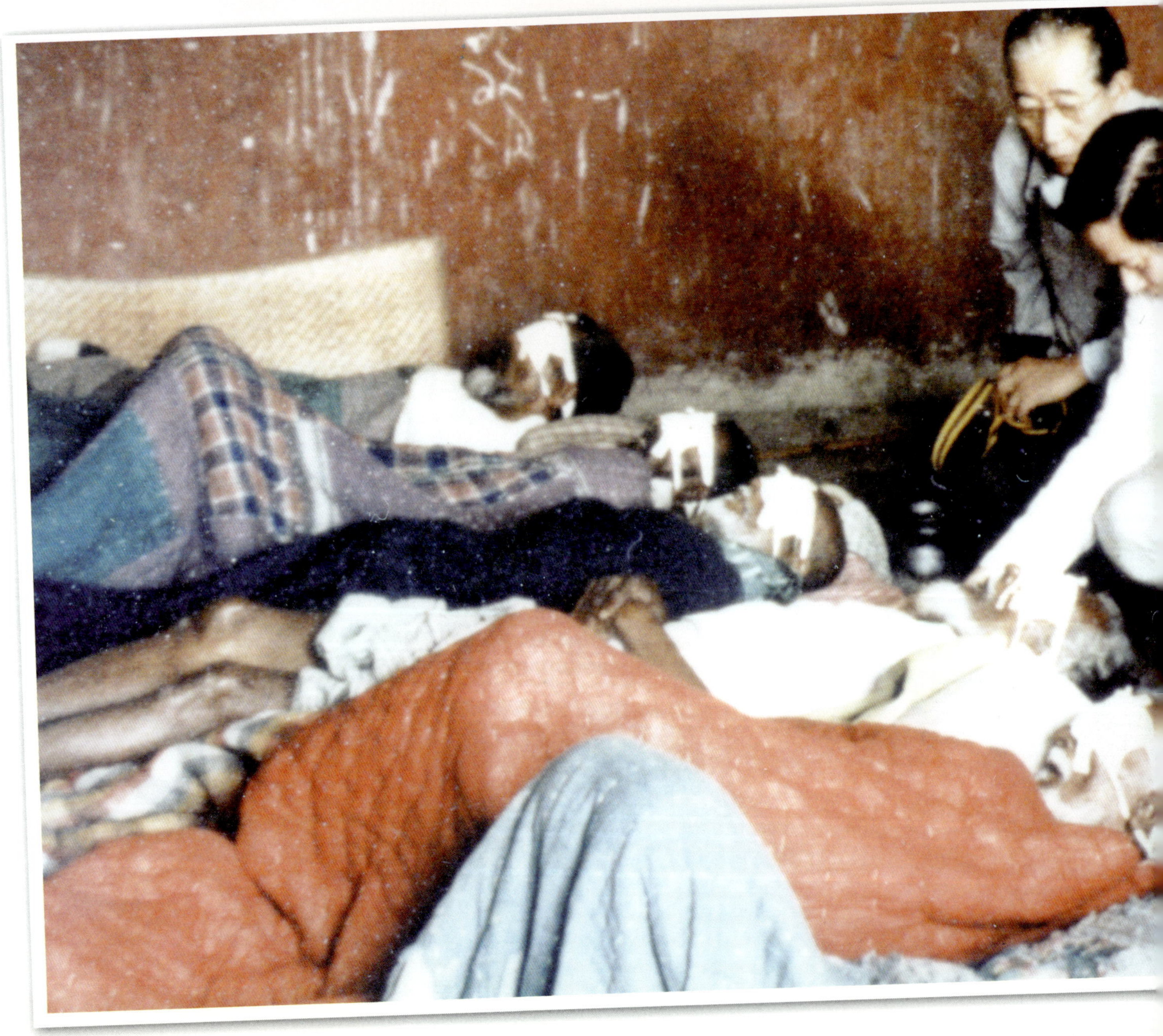

“God gave me vision, but nature took it away. You have restored my vision. To me, you’re God”

K Konyama with Arthur Lim

She'd held my hand all along and she gripped it now. "I have come so far because I have faith in you," she said simply.

I patted her hand. "Thank you. I'll do my best for you." I gave some final instructions to Miss Muthi about the operation and they left.

After my day's work at the clinic, I looked at Mrs Muthi's file. There were changes in her eyes which suggest that the operation may not turn out well. Although I had discussed the problems briefly with her and her family, I did not go into details and did not stress on the severity of some of the problems. I did not want to worry her unnecessarily. She had decided on the operation soon after I gave her a prognosis.

Thinking about this reminded me of a case in London I heard about some years ago. There was a well-known surgeon who was to operate on a BBC announcer. The night before the surgery, he assured the woman that she'd be all right, knowing very well that she might lose her voice. The surgeon had thought: what was the point of telling her that she might lose her voice? It'd only make her more anxious. Unfortunately she lost her voice after the operation, and sued the surgeon.

I've often thought about the rights of a patient to know. In the case of the BBC announcer, Lord Denning took the view that "a doctor, a surgeon may not say the truth in this case, but did he do that to protect himself or for a special reason? He did that purely for the reason that he wanted to allay the anxiety of this patient." Lord Denning also said that "a good doctor, out of the goodness of the heart, try to console patients – that is what doctoring is about, and surely when all went well, everyone was happy and no great effort was required to maintain this happiness. On the other hand, when things went wrong, time and effort must be invested to ensure understanding and acceptance of un unfortunate situation.

I read Mrs Muthi's note again. I was strangely moved by it. Her heartfelt gratitude was evident in those few lines and she had called me a god. Being called a god wasn't something I was used to, but I understood that to the Hindus, human beings could be gods.

It was a strange coincidence that in the following two months, I received more patients from India than I ever had before. Two men in particular reminded me of Mrs Muthi. After I had restored their vision, they told me that I was a god and insisted on kissing my feet. I felt quite uneasy but fascinated. "No, it's not necessary," I told them. However, they persisted in doing it.

Later, when I was at home reviewing the day's work, I thought about Mrs Muthi. Like her, the way the two Indian men expressed their gratitude moved me. For the first time in a long while, I reflected on how Singapore was surrounded by different cultures. Indeed, what was completely normal to one group may be different to the others. Calling a human being "God" was not the thing to do in some religions, but to the Hindus it was not unusual. Kneeling in front of someone and kissing his feet was not something I was used to doing, but to the Hindus it was an expression of their immense gratitude.

These incidents showed me how rich and complex our individual cultures are, and impressed me with the message that only international goodwill and understanding of our different cultures will hold the world together tomorrow.

Eye Camps in South Asia

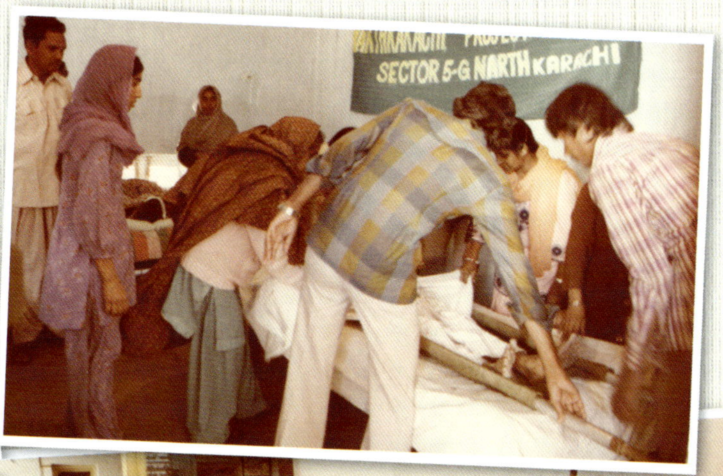

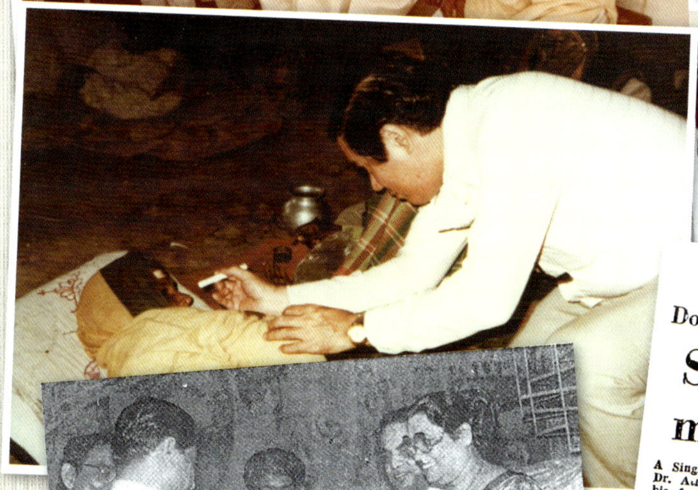

Mrs. A. J. Ranasinghe hands over 12,700 Singapore dollars (approximately Rs. 250,000) to President Premadasa at the Sucharitha on Thursday. This was the sum of money Mrs. Ranasinghe paid to Dr. Arthur Lim of Singapore when she underwent a cataract operation in Singapore recently. Dr. Lim in turn donated this money to Sri Lanka, as an initial sum to start a Training Centre for Cataract Implantation in Sri Lanka. Dr. Lim has already set up such centres in China and India. The visiting Peace Leader Sri Chinmoy promised to donate equipment to the Eye Hospital.

Among others present on the occasion were Mr. Ratnasiri Rajapakse, vice Chairman, National Water Supply and Drainage Board, Dr. Upali Mendis, Dr. Yamuna Ratnayake, Mr. Janaka B. Nakkawita, Sri Lanka's High Commissioner in Singapore and Dr. Jayalath Jayawardena.

SUN Saturday, January 6, 1990.

Donates fee for cataract centre here

Singapore eye specialist makes grand gesture

A Singaporean eye specialist Dr. Arthur Lim has donated his fee of Singapore $12,700 for the setting up of an cataract operating centre in Sri Lanka.

The money (approximately Sri Lankan Rs. 275,000) was handed over by Mrs. Seetha Ranasinghe, wife of State Minister of Information A. J. Ranasinghe who underwent the operation to President Premadasa who in turn gave the donation to Dr. Upali Mendis, Director Eye Hospital for the purpose.

The Singaporean specialist at Mount Elizabeth ...Medcal Centre had declined his fee from Mrs Ranasinghe on the grounds that there were many Sri Lankans who could not afford to pay for such operations and requested her to use the money for a centre to help them.

Shri Chinmoy who was present also promised to send medical equipment necessary for the centre.

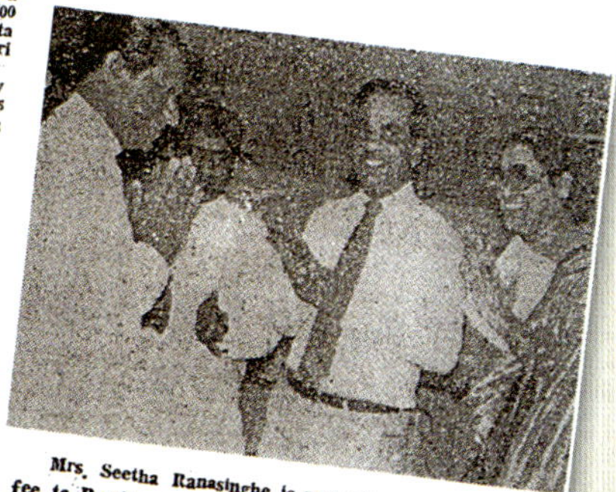

Mrs. Seetha Ranasinghe is seen after she donated the fee to President Premadasa. Secretary of the Suchari tha Movement and Deputy Chairman of the NWSDB Ratnasiri Rajapakse is also in the picture.

Cataract Blindness and Surgery

Millions of cataract patients have normal vision restored with low cost simple techniques of cataract removal. It is wrong to introduce costly high tech procedures, too costly for the neglected poor rural areas of some developing nations.

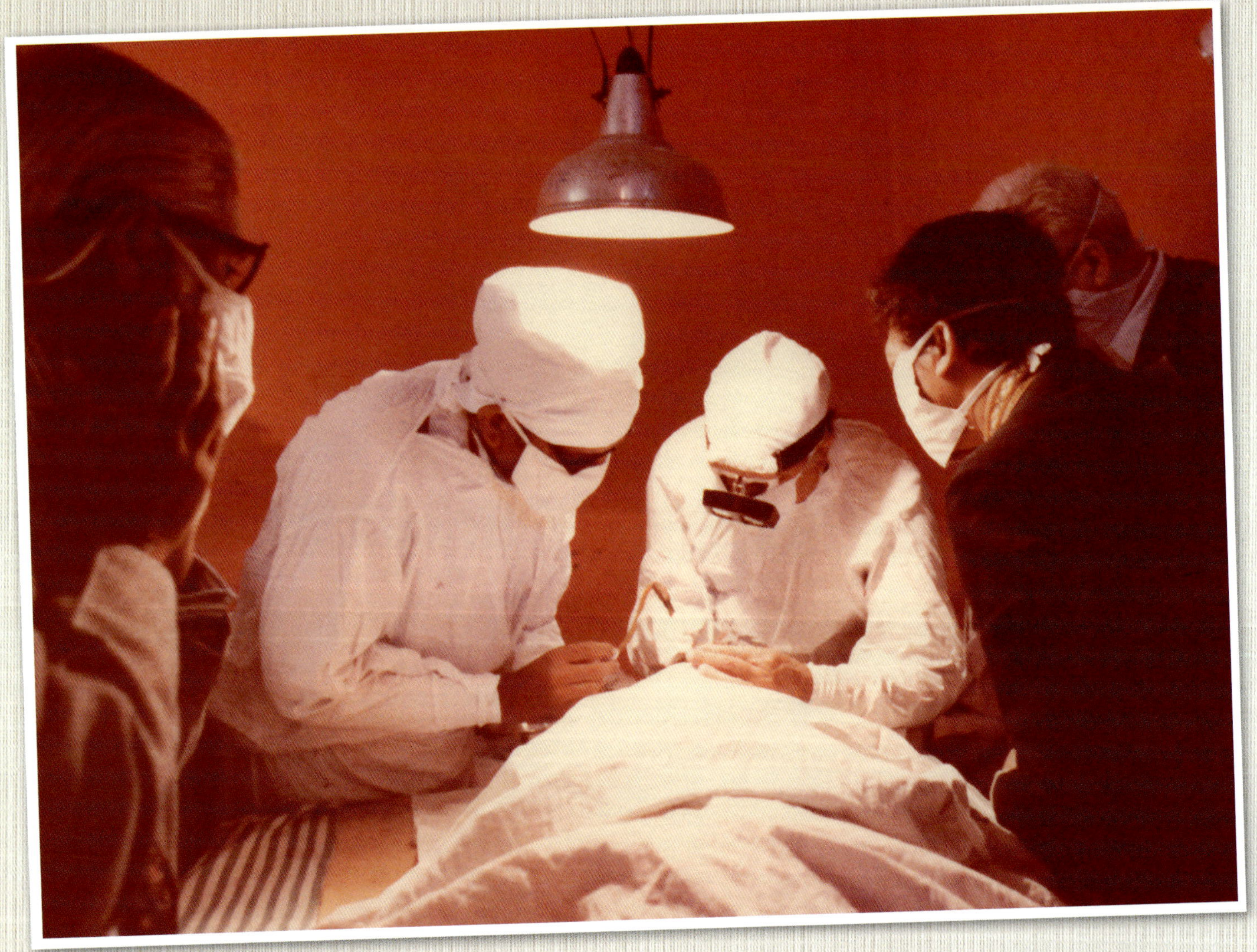

Supporting quality eye care in Sri Lanka

Success comes when the visiting surgeons work as friends and colleagues of the local surgeons, never critical of their low cost approach.

K Konyama from Japan (seated, left) and Arthur Lim from Singapore (standing, 2nd from left) mixing freely with the Bangladeshi helpers, restoring sight to thousands at their eye camps.

Cataract Blindness in China

Normal vision restored to millions of cataract victims in China where the techniques are more advanced and most received intraocular lens implant – because the People's Republic of China is wealthier.

Millions of cataract patients had normal vision restored in China

I was blind, NOW I SEE

" Millions of people are blind globally, but I face the misery of blindness on my own. It was a miracle when Professor Lim restored my vision at no cost as my family was poor."

Rokhaiyah was blind in both eyes from a severe infection that had complicated an injury. At the age of six, she was sent to the Singapore Blind School where she learnt Braille for 12 years as she could hardly see hand movements.

I met her when she was 18 when I was volunteering at the school. I noticed the light projection on her right eye was good and there was a brisk pupillary reaction to light. I felt there was a good chance her vision could be partially restored.

However, she could not afford to pay for surgery and hospital expenses. I decided to waive the surgical fee and absorb other additional costs.

We proceeded with her surgery at Mount Alvernia Hospital with help and support from Reverend Mother Superior Angela and her nurses. During surgery, we aspirated the dense cataract.

At the end of the surgery, we managed to view the fundus which showed a normal macular, indicating that Rokhaiyah would have good vision restored.

She was very tense when the dressing was removed. She opened her eyes with an excited expression of happiness, and quietly said, "Doctor, I can see."

Upon her discharge, she enjoyed vision of 6/18 with glasses. Within a week, her vision improved to 6/6 (normal

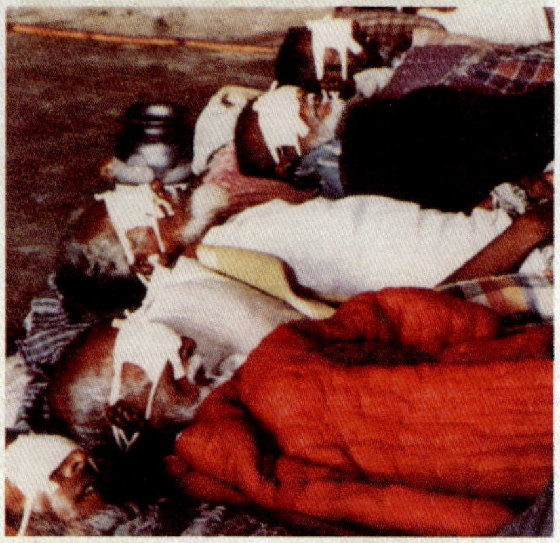

vision). Because she had some difficulties adjusting to the formula of words from letters, she continued to use Braille initially.

I had not seen Rokhaiyah for 20 years when one day she came to my clinic and said, "Doctor you won't believe that I have graduated from the Singapore Institute of Management (SIM), Singapore's fourth university.

"I am going to receive my diploma from the chancellor of SIM, Professor Cham Tao Soon. Are you not proud of me?"

I answered, "Of course... It is wonderful."

Arrangements had been made, unbeknown to me, for the press to interview her and a story was published with the touching headline, "Doctor, come see what I have achieved".

The article described how Rokhaiyah received an incredible birthday present – the gift of sight – 30 years ago. It detailed the amazing life she had led since her surgery: becoming a teacher in Sin Ming Primary, getting married and being a mother of three children, aged between 13 and 20.

In addition, she had entered the Institute of Education after her A levels and taught at a school for the blind before joining the Ministry of Education.

Her story has been tremendously gratifying to me as a doctor.

However, we can do so much more by spreading our skills and knowledge: if you do one good operation, you restore vision to one person, but if you teach hundreds of eye surgeons to perform quality cataract surgery at low cost, you can restore vision to a million blind persons.

I hope that I can contribute to restoring vision to patients throughout Asia and am particularly proud of the Cataract Training Centre in Tianjin, China, where 2,500 eye surgeons were trained in modern microsurgical cataract techniques to insert a posterior chamber implant.

Together with Chinese ophthalmologists, I am hopeful we can remove a million cataracts.

International Leaders Who Came To help

Former Health Minister of Vietnam Prof Dr Nguyen Trong Nhan, R Pararajasegaram (Sri Lanka), Ian Constable (Autralia) and K Konyama (Japan).

Rabiul Husain (Bangladesh), MA Matin (Bangladesh), K Shimizu (Japan), Saiichi Mishima (Japan), S Selvarajah (Malaysia), Madan Upadhyay (Nepal), August Deutman (Netherlands), Benjamin Boyd (Panama), Zhang Xiao-Lou (People's Republic of China) and Winifred Mao (People's Republic of China)

We are grateful to the following individuals for contributing to this special book.

To The Straits Times for permission to reproduce several articles that appear in this book.

To the NUS alumni who gave of their precious time, talents and treasures.

To the NUS Office of Alumni Relations who sponsored this publication and
Ms Chua Beng Hwee, Deputy Director, Ms Adeline Bek, Manager, Partnerships & Services,
for facilitating the contributions from the NUS graduates.

To Ms Leona Lo and Ms Gan Meng Meng for editorial support &
Ms Julie Yeong for her secretarial support.

To Mr Jeffrey Goh of SinKho Advertising & Design for his excellent design work.

And finally, to Arthur Lim & Charity Wai, our tireless editors.

Without your generous assistance, this publication would not have been possible.